THE PRINCESS CASAMASSIMA

Borgo Press Dramas by FRANK J. MORLOCK

Chuzzlewit
Crime and Punishment
Falstaff (with William Shakespeare, John Dennis, and William Kendrick)
Fathers and Sons
Notes from the Underground
Outrageous Women: Lady Macbeth and Other French Plays (editor and translator)
The Princess Casamassima
A Raw Youth
The Stendhal Hamlet Scenarios and Other Shakespearean Shorts from the French (editor and translator)

THE PRINCESS CASAMASSIMA

A PLAY IN FIVE ACTS

FRANK J. MORLOCK

Adapted from the Novel by Henry James

THE BORGO PRESS
MMXII

THE PRINCESS CASAMASSIMA

Copyright © 2012 by Frank J. Morlock

FIRST EDITION

Published by Wildside Press LLC

www.wildsidebooks.com

DEDICATION

For Milan Jurecka

CONTENTS

CAST OF CHARACTERS 9

ACT I, Scene 1 11

ACT I, Scene 2 35

ACT II, Scene 3 51

ACT II, Scene 4 62

ACT II, Scene 5 76

ACT III, Scene 6 90

ACT III, Scene 7 118

ACT IV, Scene 8 152

ACT IV, Scene 9 164

ACT IV, Scene 10 173

ACT V, Scene 11 178

ACT V, Scene 12 187

ACT V, Scene 13 196

ABOUT THE AUTHOR 210

CAST OF CHARACTERS

Pinnie

Hyacinth Robinson

Mr. Vetch

Mr. Poupin

Madame Poupin

Captain Sholto

Millicent Henning

Paul Muniment

Rosy Muniment

The Princess Casamassima

The Prince

Lady Aurora

Madame Grandoni

Seven women, six men.

ACT I

SCENE 1. PINNIE'S MILLINERY SHOP.

It is a poor seamstress's shop in a London slum about 1885. Pinnie is a middle-aged woman, very thin, and possessed of a wiry, puritanical energy. Pinnie is puzzled by the appearance of the fashionably dressed, blowsy Millicent Henning. Indeed old Pinnie is in a state of partial shock, not knowing whether to admit the girl or not, or what she can possibly want of her.

Milly

Well, you'll have to guess my name before I tell you. Won't you let me in? I don't want to order anything, I only came to inquire after your 'ealth. Now, tell me, how's old Hyacinth? I should like so much to see him.

Pinnie

Old Hyacinth?

Milly

Perhaps you call him Mr. Robinson today—you always wanted him to hold himself so high. But to his face I'll call him the way I always did, you wait and see.

Pinnie

Bless my soul, you must be that awful little 'Enning girl!

Milly (indignant)

Well! I'm glad you finally recognized me. I suppose I was awful. (brightly) But, I ain't so bad now, hey? I has a call to make in these parts, and it came into my 'ead to look you up. I don't forget old friends.

Pinnie

You've improved as I couldn't have believed.

Milly

Well—you haven't changed. You were always calling me something 'orrid.

Pinnie

I daresay it doesn't matter to you now, does it?

Milly

Oh, I'm all right now.

Pinnie

You were a pretty child— I never said contrary to that. But I had no idea you'd turn out like this. You're too tall for a woman.

Milly

Well, I enjoy beautiful 'ealth. Everyone thinks I'm at least twenty-two.

Pinnie

But how did you get so splendid?

Milly

Laws! Just luck. I got work as a shop girl in a fashionable store and now they use me as a model. We have to be beautifully dressed—I love to look nice.

Pinnie

And how are your parents?

Milly

Gone to 'Ell, I'm afraid. They drifted off years ago, and I'm on my own.

Pinnie (suspiciously)

You haven't come here to see me.

Milly

I'm glad to see you. I told you I came to ask after my sweetheart. Wot's become of him?

Pinnie

He's an apprentice bookbinder.

Milly

In bookbinding? Laws! Do you mean he works? Well, I always knew he would have something to do with books. But, I didn't think he would ever follow a trade.

Pinnie

A trade? Mr. Robinson considers it one of the fine arts.

Milly

Very likely it's good work. Better than this, no doubt.

Pinnie (crossly)

I haven't so much work as I used to have, if that's what you mean. My eyes aren't so good and neither is my health these days.

Milly

You need some new ideas about fashion. You need someone to help you. I can see you're using the same old styles as ever.

Pinnie

I've had helpers in the past. None of them turned out any good.

Milly

Maybe I can get you some business—you always did excellent sewing—but, you ain't got no sense of fashion. I'll bring the patterns.

Pinnie (some sense of Pinnie's poverty can be gained from the fact that she would like to reject such help out of hand but swallows her pride and says quietly)

That would be very kind.

Milly

Mind you give my love to Hyacinth. I don't care if you know that the only reason I stopped was in hope of seeing him again. There's no shame in wanting to see my childhood sweetheart. Do give him my best love, and tell him I hope he'll come and see me. I can see you won't tell him anything. What are you afraid of? I won't hurt your precious Hyacinth. I'll leave my card for him all the same. (extracting a visiting card from her purse)

Pinnie (amazed at the little Henning girl's social standing without being in any way delighted by it)

My word!

Milly

What do you think I want to do with him? I could swallow him in one bite.

Pinnie

You needn't think I shall put myself out to keep him in the dark. I shall certainly tell him you've been here, and exactly how you strike me.

Milly

Of course, you'll say something nasty like you used to when I was a child. You used to let me 'ave it then, you know.

Pinnie

Ah, well, you're very different now, when I think what you've come from.

Milly

What I've come from? Just because you're stuck in this slum, don't expect me to stay 'ere! You've had to stay in it yourself, so you might speak civilly of it! And pray, what have you come from yourself, and what has he come from? The mysterious Mr. Hyacinth Robinson, whose father was Lord Fredrick and whose mother was—

Pinnie (jumping up)

I've nothing to tell you. Leave my shop!

(Hyacinth Robinson, a finely built, young man of about twenty enters unseen by Pinnie, but visible to Millicent.)

Milly

Gracious, Hyacinth Robinson—is that you?

(Pinnie turns around, then immediately, crestfallen, goes to her sewing desk.)

Hyacinth

Were you talking about me just now?

Milly

When I asked where you 'ad come from? (innocently) That was because we heard you in the 'all. I suppose you've come from your work.

Hyacinth

You used to live in the Place—you were the girl that always wanted to kiss me. Didn't she live in Lomax Place, Pinnie?

Milly

Do you know what you look like—you look for all the world like a plastered up Frenchman! Don't he look like a funny little Frenchie, Mrs. Pysnet?

Hyacinth

Have you come back to live in the Place?

Milly

Heaven forbid, that I should ever do that! I must live near the establishment in which I am employed.

Hyacinth

And what establishment is that now? Is it the Cock and Bull, or the Elephant and Castle?

Milly

A pub? Well, you haven't got the manners of a Frenchie.

Pinnie (under her breath)

Whorehouse more likely!

Milly

I don't care what a man looks like so long as he knows a lot. That's the look I like.

Pinnie

Miss 'Enning wouldn't live in Lomax Place for the world. She thinks it too low.

Hyacinth

So it is, it's a beastly hole.

Milly

Right you are!

Hyacinth

Don't you think I know something?

Milly

You? Oh, I don't care a straw what you know!

Pinnie

I think you had better shut the door.

Hyacinth

Did you come here on purpose to see us?

Milly

I thought I'd just give it a look. I had an engagement not far off. But I wouldn't have believed anyone who said I'd find you just where I left you.

Pinnie (sourly)

We needed you to look after us!

Hyacinth

Oh, you're such a success.

Milly

None of your rattling impudence. I'm as good a girl as there is in London. If you were to offer to see me home, I'd tell you I don't knock about that way with gentlemen.

Hyacinth

I'll go with you as far as you like.

Milly

Well—all right—but it's only because I knew you as a baby.

Hyacinth

Pinnie, let's have some tea.

(Pinnie, mortified, obeys and goes out to get the tea.)

Milly

What a way to treat your mother. Oh—I forgot she ain't your mother. How stupid I am! I keep forgetting.

Hyacinth

My mother died many years ago; she was an invalid. But Pinnie has been very good to me.

Milly

My mother's dead, too. She died very suddenly. I daresay you remember her in the Place. But I've had no Pinnie.

Hyacinth

You look as if you can take care of yourself.

Milly

Well, I'm very healthy. What became of Mr. Vetch? We used to say that if Miss Pysnet was your mama, Mr. Vetch was your papa. We used to call him Miss Pysnet's young man.

Hyacinth

He's her young man still. He's our best friend. He lives by his fiddle—as he used to. In fact, he got me the place I'm now in.

Milly

I should have thought he would get you a place at his theatre.

Hyacinth

At his theatre? But, I'd be no use in the theatre. I don't play any instrument.

Milly

I don't mean in the orchestra, you baby. You'd look very nice in a fancy costume. Is Miss Pysnet some relation? What gave her any rights over you?

Hyacinth (uneasily)

Miss Pysnet's an old friend of the family. My mother was very fond of her and she was fond of my mother. Mr. Vetch has changed his lodgings: he moved out of Seventeen three years ago. He couldn't stand the other people in the house. There was a man who played the accordion.

Milly (reproachfully)

He might have put you into something better than a bookbinder's.

Hyacinth

He wasn't obliged to put me into anything. After all, he's not even a relation of Pinnie's. And he has trouble enough supporting himself. I think he never married Pinnie—assuming he could persuade her—because he has no money.

(Pinnie returns with the teapot and servings. After placing everything on the table, she stalks out.)

Milly

Friendly, ain't she?

Hyacinth

She's very protective of me. She's always afraid I'll marry beneath me.

Milly

All the same, I didn't expect to find you in a bookbinder's.

Hyacinth

Where would you have looked to find me? Pity you couldn't have told me in advance, I'd have endeavored to meet your expectations.

Milly

Do you know what they used to say in the Place? They say your father was a Lord. A real English Lord.

Hyacinth

Very likely. That's the kind of gossip they spread in that precious hole.

Milly

Well, perhaps he was.

Hyacinth

He might have been Prime Minister for all the good it has done me.

Milly

Fancy, your talking as if you didn't know!

Hyacinth (politely, but savagely)

Finish your tea. Don't mind how I talk.

Milly

Well, you 'ave got a temper. I should've thought you'd be a clerk to a lawyer, or at a bank.

Hyacinth

Do they select them for their tempers?

Milly

You know what I mean. You used to be so clever. I never thought you'd follow a trade.

Hyacinth

I'm not clever enough to live on air.

Milly

You might be, really, for all the tea you drink! Why didn't you go in for some profession?

Hyacinth (bitterly)

How was I to go in? Who the devil was to help me?

Milly

Haven't you got a connection?

Hyacinth

Are you trying to trick me into boasting of my aristocratic connections? Sorry, I don't have any.

Milly

Well, I'm sorry you're only a journeyman.

Hyacinth

So am I! But the art of bookbinding is an exquisite art, I'll say that. Even if it doesn't pay well.

Milly

So Pinnie told me! Have you got some samples? I'd like to look at some.

Hyacinth (condescendingly)

You wouldn't know how good they are.

Milly (irritated)

That's just the way you used to talk to me years ago in the Place.

Hyacinth

I don't care about that. I hate all that time.

Milly

If you come to that, so do I! You always used to have your nose in a book. I never thought you'd work with your hands.

Hyacinth

Depend upon it, I won't do it an hour longer than I have to.

Milly

What will you do then?

Hyacinth

You'll see someday. I had to do something. I couldn't go on living off Pinnie. I took what I could get. Thank God I help her a little now.

Milly

You talk like a reg'lar gentleman.

Hyacinth

I'm not. I'm just an obscure little beggar born of a French woman to a supposed English Lord—living in a squalid little corner of London. And so, I'm a bookbinder.

Milly

I didn't think I could ever fancy anyone in that line.

Hyacinth

Allow me to see you out.

Milly

I should be delighted. (aside) A reg'lar gentleman.

(Exit Milly and Hyacinth out the street door. After a moment, enter Mr. Vetch with Poupin, Madame Poupin, and Paul Muniment.)

Vetch

Pinnie was good enough to let us meet here.

(They close the shutters. Poupin coughs terribly, and is helped by his wife.)

Vetch

Are you all right, my dear Poupin?

Poupin

I'm suffering extremely, but we must all suffer so long as the social question is so abominably, iniquitously neglected.

Madame

Ah yes, the politicians never think of the poor. There are times when I ask myself how long it will go on.

Poupin (passionately)

It will go on till the measure of their infamy is full. Till the day of justice! Till the day the disinherited shake the globe!

Madame

Oh, we always see things continue; we never see them change.

Poupin

We may not see it, but They will see it.

Paul

What do you mean, shake the globe?

Poupin

I mean that force will make the bourgeoisie go down to their cellars and hide—behind their barrels of wine and their heaps of gold.

(Hyacinth quietly reenters; he is expected and the discussion continues without interruption. Someone says "You're late.")

Madame

And, in this country, I hope in their coal bins. La, la, we shall find them even there.

Poupin

Eighty-nine was an irresistible force.

Paul

Yes, I know, I know you fought them. But everything is yet to be tried.

Poupin

Oh, the trial will be on a grand scale. *Soyez tranquille.*

Madame (indicating Hyacinth and Paul)

You ought to present these gentlemen.

Poupin

Monsieur Hyacinth is a gifted child—a child in whom I take a tender interest—a child who has an account to settle. Oh, a thumping big one! Isn't that so, *mon petit*?

Hyacinth

Oh, I only want them to leave me alone.

Poupin

He's very young.

Madame

He's the person we have seen in this country that we like the best.

Paul

Perhaps he's French.

Hyacinth

Oh, I'm nothing.

Madame

Do you mean to say you're not as good as anyone else in this world? I should like to see—!

Paul

We all have an account to settle, don't you know?

Madame

It is a shame not to take Monsieur Hyacinth in.

Poupin

All in good time, all in good time. Monsieur Hyacinth knows that I count on him, whether I make him an intern today or tomorrow.

Hyacinth

What do you mean "intern"?

Poupin

Do not trifle with state secrets. You are too young.

Madame

One is never too young to do one's bit.

Paul

Can you keep a secret?

Hyacinth

Is it a plot? A conspiracy?

Poupin

He asks as if he were asking for plum pudding. It's terribly serious, my child.

Paul

It's a group of workers to which he (indicating Poupin) and I, and a good many others belong. (Poupin scowls) There's no harm in telling him that.

Madame

I advise you not to tell it to Miz Pinnie; she's quite in the old ideas.

Vetch

I quite agree. Pinnie thinks we are merely having a social gathering.

Hyacinth

If you've got some plan, something to which one can give one's self— I think you might tell me.

Poupin

It's an accident you haven't met Paul here before.

Madame

How could they have met, when Mr. Paul never comes? He doesn't spoil us!

Paul (seriously)

Well, you see, I have my little sister at home to take care of. This afternoon, luckily, a lady came to sit with her.

Madame

A lady—a real lady?

Paul

Oh yes, every inch a lady.

Madame

Why do you permit them to thrust themselves in on you, simply because you have the misfortune to be poor? It seems to be the custom in this country—but it wouldn't suit me, or any other person from France at all. I should like to see one of *ces dames*, one of the real ones, coming to sit with me.

Paul

Oh, you're not a cripple. You've got the use of your legs, whereas Rosy—

Madame

Yes, and my tongue!

Paul

This lady looks after several others in our tenement—and reads to my sister.

Madame

It would enrage me! You are too patient, you English.

Paul

We need patience. We shall never do anything without that.

Poupin

You're perfectly right about that. You cannot say it too often. It will be a tremendous job. Only the strong will prevail.

Paul (to Hyacinth)

Madame says we ought to know each other—

Hyacinth

Will you tell me all about your plot?

Paul (warily)

It's not a plot. I don't care much for plots. It's just taking a stand on two or three points.

Poupin

A stand, that's what we must make—a stand! (he begins coughing terribly)

Madame

Between us, we've thrown him into a fever. We'd better go.

Paul (to Hyacinth as the Poupins prepare to leave with Vetch)

My mane is Paul—

Hyacinth

And what's your trade?

Paul

I work for a firm of wholesale chemists at Lambeth.

Hyacinth

And where do you live?

Paul

On the far side of London. The south actually.

Hyacinth

Are you going home now?

Paul

Yes, I'm going to toddle.

Hyacinth

And may I toddle with you?

Paul

If you like, but you won't learn about any plots. Still coming?

Hyacinth

Yes.

Paul

Come along. You can meet my sister,—her name's Rosy. You've never met anyone like her.

BLACKOUT

ACT I
Scene 2. Rosy's bedroom.

The room is dark.

Paul (from outside)

Hallo, have you gone to roost?

Rosy

Oh dear, no: we're sitting in the dark. Lady Aurora's so kind. She's still here.

(Lady Aurora lights a lamp. Rosy is revealed in bed.)

Paul (entering with Hyacinth)

Well now, that's beautiful. You'll have a party then, for I've brought someone else. We're poor, you know, but honest, and not afraid of showing up. We can manage a candle.

Aurora

Oh, I brought some candles; we could have a light if you wished.

Paul

Rosy, girl, I've brought you a visitor. This young man has walked all the way from Lisson Grove to make your acquaintance. (to Hyacinth) You mustn't mind her being in bed—she's always in bed. Just the way a slippery little trout's in the water.

Rosy

Dear me, if I didn't receive company because I was in bed, there wouldn't be much use, would there, Lady Aurora?

Aurora

Oh, mercy, no; it seems quite the natural place! And it's such a lovely bed, such a comfortable bed.

Rosy

Indeed it is, when your Ladyship makes it up.

Paul (to Lady Aurora)

You haven't been doing that again?

Aurora

Who would if I didn't? It only takes a minute if someone knows how.

Paul

I can do it well enough.

Aurora

Oh, I've no doubt whatever.

Paul

This is Mr. Hyacinth Robinson. That won't tell you much, but you'll like him; he's all right. I was introduced by the Poupins.

Rosy

Your name, like mine, represents a flower. Mine is Rose Muniment, and her Ladyship is Aurora Langrish. That means the morning or the dawn; it's the most beautiful of all, don't you think? Isn't it right she should be called dawn when she brings light wherever she goes? The Poupins are the charming foreigners I've told you about. (this last to Lady Aurora)

Aurora

Oh, it's so pleasant knowing a few foreigners. They're often so fresh.

Paul

Mr. Robinson's a sort of foreigner—and he's definitely fresh. Speaks French very well.

Aurora

Oh, there are so many good books in French.

Hyacinth

Rather a torment when you have no way of getting at them.

Aurora

Well, I have a good deal of my own, and I should be glad to give you some.

Hyacinth

Well, thank you very much.

Rosy

Isn't that just like her ladyship—wanting to make up to people for being less lucky than herself. She'd take the shoes off her feet for anyone that might take a fancy to them.

Aurora

I'll stop coming to see you, if you're going to take me up like this for everything. It's the least I can do—to give what I have.

Rosy

Lady Aurora is ashamed of being rich. She's a tremendous socialist. Worse even than Paul.

Hyacinth

I wonder if she's worse than me?

Paul

Hullo, I didn't know you were so advanced. Have we been entertaining an angel unawares?

Hyacinth

You didn't know I was so advanced? Why, I thought that was the principal thing about me.

Paul

I thought the principal thing about you was that you knew French.

Aurora

I should like so very much to know—it would be interesting—how far exactly you do go?

Hyacinth

I think I go about as far as anybody. I think I see my way to conclusions from which even the Poupins would shrink. Poupin, at any rate—I'm not so sure about his wife.

Aurora

I should like so much to know her.

Paul

The principal conclusion Mr. Robinson sees his way to is that your father ought to have his head chopped off and carried on a pike.

Aurora

Ah, yes. The French Revolution.

Hyacinth

I don't know anything about your father.

Rosy

Didn't you ever hear of Lord Inglefield?

Aurora

He's one of the best.

Paul

Very likely, but he's a landlord with a park of five thousand acres all to himself, while we're bundled together in a sort of kennel.

Rosy

I've told you often enough that I don't go along with you at all.

Paul

Everything points to great changes in the country, but if once our Rosy's against them—how can we be sure?

Rosy

Her Ladyship may think I'm as good as her—but she can't make me believe it.

Aurora

I think you're much better than I—and I know very few people as good as you. Apropos of revolution—if there were to be a—

disturbance—I believe the upper classes would behave quite differently. I don't think they'd all go abroad.

Hyacinth

Go abroad?

Aurora

I mean they'd stay and resist. They'd fight very hard.

Rosy

I'm sure they'd win, too.

Aurora

They'd struggle until they were beaten.

Hyacinth

And you think they'd be beaten in the end?

Aurora

Oh, yes. But I hope it won't come to that.

Paul

I infer you all talk it over amongst yourselves—to settle the line you'll take.

Rosy

But I detect something in her tone which I think is a great mistake. If her Ladyship thinks to be let off easily for the concession she's made in advance—she can save herself the trouble. The people won't be a bit wiser. They won't know or care. So don't waste your time or good nature. When you're up so high as that you've got to stay there. The best thing you can do is hold up your head! I can promise your Ladyship I would.

Paul

Rosy's right, my Lady. It's no use trying to buy yourself off. You can't do enough. Eat your pudding while you have it—you may not have it long.

Aurora

You're the most delightful people. I wish everyone could know you. But I must really be going.

Rosy

Paul will see you as far as you like.

Aurora

Well, you may see me down stairs.

Rosy

You must call a cab.

Aurora

Oh, I don't go in cabs. I walk.

Paul

Well, you may go on top of a bus if you like. You can't help being superb.

Aurora

Superb? Oh, mercy!

Paul (following Lady Aurora out)

Wait for me a little.

(Exit Aurora, followed by Paul.)

Rosy (to Hyacinth)

She lives in Belgrave Square; she has ever so many brothers and sisters; one of her sisters is married to Lord Warmington— She's dedicated her life to the poor. And she's so natural. She's not the least condescending.

Hyacinth

No, she's not. (pause) You and your brother strike me as being very curious people.

Rosy

Really! If you had known my father and mother—

Hyacinth

Were they curious, too?

Rosy

Rather. They came from the mines. My father was working in a pit when he was a child of ten. He never had a day's schooling in his life, but he invented a machine. My father was as black as the coal he worked. But he was intelligent, my mother, too. But, what's the use of brains if you haven't got a backbone? He invented a new kind of beam fixing device—whatever that is. And he sold it for fifteen pounds. No royalties! Nothing. He used to get drunk. He fell into a gravel pit. That's the reason my brother won't touch a drop. My mother kept us decent somehow. She was terribly handsome. And it was from her we got our education. She did it somehow. Then she was taken by typhoid. Our parents had good brains to give us.

Hyacinth

Are you very fond of your brother?

Rosy

If you ever quarrel with him, you'll see whose side I shall take.

Hyacinth

Before that, I'll take care to make you like me.

Rosy

I already do. But, see how fast I'll fling you over.

Hyacinth

Then, why are you so opposed to his ideas?

Rosy

He'll get over them.

Hyacinth

Never! I've only known him for a day—but I can tell!

Rosy

Is that the way you're going to make me like you—by contradicting me so?

Hyacinth

You don't believe in human equality?

Rosy

I haven't the least objection to seeing the people improved—but I don't want to see the aristocracy lowered even an inch.

Hyacinth

Positively feudal. You ought to know my aunt Pinnie. She's another idolater of the aristocracy.

Rosy

Oh, you're making me like you very fast! And pray, who's your aunt Pinnie?

Hyacinth

She's a dressmaker. I'll bring her someday. Don't you want a better place to live in?

Rosy

A better place than this? How could there be a better place than this? If you think I'm not perfectly content, you're very much mistaken.

Hyacinth

Don't you sometimes make your brother very cross?

Rosy

Cross? Never with me.

Hyacinth

Isn't he deep in—

Rosy

Deep in what?

Hyacinth

Doesn't he belong to important things?

Rosy

You must ask him. I don't know.

(Paul reenters.)

Rosy (to Paul)

You must have crossed the Channel with her Ladyship. I wonder which of you enjoyed the walk most?

Paul

She's a handy old girl, and has a goodish stride.

Rosy

I think she's in love with you.

Paul

Really, my dear, for an admirer of the aristocracy, you allow yourself a license.

Hyacinth

Perhaps she is—why not?

Paul

She's daft enough for anything.

Hyacinth

But, is she only playing, or is she in earnest?

Paul (changing the subject)

How are you two getting on?

Rosy (ironically)

Oh, he's made himself most agreeable.

Hyacinth

She won't tell me about your revolutionary clubs.

Paul

You mustn't ask her that sort of thing.

Hyacinth

What can I do if you won't tell me anything definite yourself?

Rosy

It will be definite enough when you get hanged for it.

Paul

Why do you want to poke your head into ugly black holes?

Hyacinth

Don't you belong to the party of action?

Paul

Where did you pick up that catchword? In the newspapers? Is that the party you want to belong to?

Hyacinth

Yes. Show me the thing.

Paul

What thing do you mean, infatuated, deluded youth?

Rosy

Well, you do go places you had far better keep out of. I wonder, sometimes, when they are going to make a search for your papers.

Paul

The day they find my papers, my dear, will be the day you get up and dance.

Hyacinth

What did you ask me to come here for?

Paul

To see if you'd be afraid.

Hyacinth

Try me.

Rosy

I'm sure if you introduce him to some of your low, wicked friends, he'll be delighted.

Hyacinth

Just the sort I want to know.

Paul

Meet me sometime.

Hyacinth

Where?

Paul

Oh, I'll tell you when we get away from her.

BLACKOUT

ACT II
Scene 3. Pinnie's shop

Hyacinth and Pinnie are talking.

Pinnie

There's only one thing I want to know. Does she expect you to marry her, dearest?

Hyacinth

Does who expect me?

Pinnie

Of course you know who I mean. The one that came after you from the other end of London—and picked you right up. Aren't there plenty of low fellows in that vulgar part where she lives—without her ravaging over here? Why can't she stick to her own beat, I should like to know? Just promise me this, my precious child—if you get into any sort of mess with that piece, you'll immediately confide it to your poor old Pinnie.

Hyacinth

My poor old Pinnie sometimes makes my quite sick. What sort of mess do you expect me to get into?

Pinnie

Suppose she pretends you promised to marry her?

Hyacinth

You don't know what you're talking about. She doesn't want to marry anyone.

Pinnie (unconvinced)

Then, what does she want?

Hyacinth

Oh, my protection.

Pinnie

Protection! Stuff. And pray, who's to protect you?

Hyacinth

In any event, it isn't from Milly that any harm will come to me.

Pinnie

I can't think why you like her.

Hyacinth

You're a good person and yet you're ready——

Pinnie

Well, what am I ready to do? I'm not ready to see you gobbled up before my eyes.

Hyacinth

You needn't be afraid of her dragging me to the altar.

Pinnie

Doesn't she think you're good enough for a 'Enning?

Hyacinth

You just don't understand. One of these days, she'll marry a very rich, very respectable alderman.

Pinnie

That creature?

Hyacinth

Or a banker, or a bishop. She doesn't want to end her career—she wants to begin it.

Pinnie

Well, I wish she'd leave you alone.

Hyacinth

What are you afraid of? Look, we'd better clear this up, once and for all. Are you afraid of my marrying a shop girl?

Pinnie (horrified)

Oh, you wouldn't, would you?

Hyacinth

The kind of girl who'd look at me is the kind of girl I'd never look at.

Pinnie

I'm sure a Princess might look at you, and be none the worse.

Hyacinth

Well, it's always nice to have your support.

Pinnie

You must be aware how lacking she is. Doesn't she bore you?

Hyacinth

She does—to extinction.

Pinnie

Then why do you spend every evening with her?

Hyacinth

What else should I do? Go to a gin palace?

Pinnie

Oh well, if you see her as she is, I don't care what you do, but try not to get her pregnant!

(Hyacinth is stunned. Enter Mr. Vetch.)

Vetch

Hallo, Pinnie.

Pinnie

Oh, Mr. Vetch, please talk some sense into him. I cannot.

(Exit Pinnie.)

Hyacinth

I haven't seen you in a long time.

Vetch

What's bothering Pinnie?

Hyacinth

I want to take a young lady to the theatre.

Vetch

I'm afraid you'll find your young lady expensive.

Hyacinth

I find everything expensive.

Vetch

Especially, I suppose, your secret societies?

Hyacinth

What do you mean by that?

Vetch

Why, you told me a while back you were about to join a few.

Hyacinth

A few? How many do you suppose? Do you think if I'd been serious, I'd tell?

Vetch

Oh dear, oh dear. (as to Milly) You want to take her to my place, I suppose?

Hyacinth

She won't go there. She wants to see something in the Strand. The Pear of Paraguay. I don't wish to pay anything if I can avoid it. I'm sorry to say I haven't a penny. But it occurred to me you might be able to get me a seat as a favor.

Vetch

Do you want a box?

Hyacinth

Something more modest.

Vetch

Why not a box?

Hyacinth

Because I haven't the clothes people wear in that sort of place.

Vetch

Your young lady has the clothes?

Hyacinth

She has everything.

Vetch

Where does she get 'em?

Hyacinth

Oh, she's a model in a high fashion shop.

Vetch (pulling out some tobacco)

Won't you have a pipe? What will she do with you?

Hyacinth

What do you mean?

Vetch

Your big amazon—Miss Henning. I know all about her from Pinnie.

Hyacinth

Then, you know my terrible fate.

Vetch

But it doesn't matter much.

Hyacinth

I don't know what you're talking about.

Vetch

Well now—the other thing. You're very deep into that.

Hyacinth

Did Pinnie tell you all about that?

Vetch

No, our friend Poupin had told me a good deal. Besides, I see it.

Hyacinth

How do you see it, pray?

Vetch

Anyone can tell to look at you, you've taken a blood oath to some cutthroat crew.

Hyacinth

You won't get me the tickets, then?

Vetch

My dear boy, I offer you a box.

Hyacinth

It has nothing to do with—

Vetch

Is it a more deadly secret?

Hyacinth

I thought you pretended to be a radical?

Vetch

Well—so I do—of the old fashioned constitutional sort. I'm not an exterminator.

Hyacinth

We don't know what we may be when the time comes.

Vetch

Is the time coming, then, my dear young friend?

Hyacinth

I don't think I can give you any more of a warning than that.

Vetch

It's very kind of you to do so much, I'm sure. Meanwhile, in the little time that is left, you wish to crowd in all possible enjoyment with the young ladies—a very natural inclination. Do you see many foreigners?

Hyacinth

Yes. A good many.

Vetch

And what do you think of them?

Hyacinth

I rather like the English best.

Vetch

Paul Muniment, for example?

Hyacinth

What do you know about him?

Vetch

I see him at the Poupins. I know you and he are thick as thieves.

Hyacinth

He'll distinguish himself very much someday.

Vetch

Very likely, very likely. And what will he do with you?

Hyacinth

Try to get me two good places in the second balcony.

Vetch (uneasily)

You had better put in all the fun you can, you know.

BLACKOUT

ACT II
Scene 4. The Lobby of a Theatre

There are several couples talking. Hyacinth and Milly enter, followed at a distance by Sholto.

Milly

Who is that man watching you?

Hyacinth

Watching me? You more likely.

Milly

Of course, he's noticed me. But you're the one he wants to get hold of.

Hyacinth

To get hold of?

Milly

Yes, you ninny, don't hang back. He may make your fortune.

Hyacinth

Well, if you'd like to meet him, I'll go and take a walk in the Strand.

Milly (after Sholto has smiled at Hyacinth) Now, do you say it's only me he's after?

Hyacinth

I'm only the pretext.

Milly

Well, if he knows us, he might give us some sign—and if he doesn't, he might leave us alone. Is he one of your grand relations? Well, I can stare as well as him. Is he one of those Lords your aunt Pinnie was talking about at the Place? No, he's too young to be your grandfather.

Hyacinth

I have no idea whether he was one of that lot.

Milly

You might at least tell me his name, so that I shall know what to call him if he comes round to speak to us.

Hyacinth

He won't do that.

Milly

He couldn't grin more if he was your own brother. He may want to make my acquaintance—after all, he wouldn't be the first.

Hyacinth

I don't know that I'm at liberty to disclose his name. I met him at a place he may not like to have it known he goes.

Milly

Do you go to places that people are ashamed of? One of your filthy political clubs, no doubt. My Lord! He is coming——

Sholto (coming over, beaming at Hyacinth)

My dear fellow, I really had to come round to speak to you. The trouble is I'm with a pair of ladies, and one of them has a great desire to make your acquaintance.

Hyacinth

To make my acquaintance?

Milly

Is that so?

Sholto

She has a tremendous desire to meet someone who looks at the whole business from your standpoint, don't you see? And in her position she scarcely has a chance. She's really the most remarkable woman in Europe.

Milly

That's all very well, but who's to look after me?

Sholto

My dear young lady, can you think I've been unmindful of that?

Milly (somewhat shocked)

I'm much obliged to you! Mr. Robinson, is it your intention to leave me? Who is the lady?

Sholto

The Princess Casamassima.

Milly

Laws! And what's she want with him?

Sholto

To discuss the lower orders.

Milly (infuriated)

And does she think we belong to them? (to Hyacinth) I don't care if you go. I should like to know about this Princess.

Sholto

Oh, I'll tell you all about her.

(Sholto escorts them off. After a slight pause, followed by a slight dimming of the lights. Hyacinth returns with the Princess Casamassima and Madame Grandoni, a very old lady of impeccable manners.)

Princess

I like to know all sorts of people.

Hyacinth

I shouldn't think you'd have any difficulty in that.

Princess

Everyone isn't so obliging as you.

Grandoni

She makes everyone do everything.

Princess

Her name is Madame Grandoni.

Grandoni

But I'm not Italian—any more than she is. She's an American, I'm actually a German. Nobody with an Italian name is Italian these days. That is a very charming person you were with.

Princess

Yes, she's very charming. We take a great interest in the things you care for. We take a great interest in the people.

Grandoni

Speak for yourself. I take none. I don't understand the people and I know nothing about them. I always respect decent people of any class, but I don't pretend any passion for the ignorant masses—because I don't have such a passion.

Princess

She lives with me; she's everything to me. She's the best woman in the world. But she has a disturbing habit of speaking her mind. What do you think of Captain Sholto?

Hyacinth

I hardly know him.

Princess

Isn't he a very curious type?

Hyacinth

Possibly. I can't make him out.

Princess

Neither can I. He's what they call a cosmopolitan. He told me he's had some interesting talks with you about the social question. That's why I asked him to introduce me.

Hyacinth

He managed to slip off with Milly very neatly.

Princess

Do you ever admit women?

Hyacinth

I'm afraid I don't understand?

Princess

Into your meetings. I should like so much to be present. Why not?

Hyacinth

I haven't seen any ladies— You know I'm not sure he should go about reporting our meetings.

Princess

I see. Perhaps you think he's a police spy or agent provocateur?

Hyacinth

No. Spies are more discreet. But, after all, he's heard very little.

Princess

You mean he hasn't really been behind the scenes? But you needn't have the least fear of Captain Sholto. He's incapable of betraying anyone. Actually, he's gone into this sort of thing merely to please me. You see, for a woman it's so difficult. So, I commissioned the Captain, ha, ha. What I wanted him to do was to make friends with the leading spirit.

Hyacinth

Surely, Captain Sholto doesn't take me for a leading spirit?

Princess

He said you were very original.

Hyacinth (laughing ironically)

I'm one of thousands in my class—there's nothing original about me at all. I am a mere particle in the grey immensity of the people.

Princess

Much more than that, I think.

Hyacinth

I have a friend who's remarkable.

Princess

Who's your friend?

Grandoni

Ah, Christina, Christina!

Hyacinth

A young man who lives in Camberwell.

Princess

Can you bring him to see me?

Hyacinth

I don't know if he would come. He might think you a little too avid for his company.

Princess

That makes me want to see him all the more. But you'll come yourself?

Hyacinth

You want me to come and see you? An unexpected honor.

Grandoni

Go and see her—go and see her once or twice. She'll treat you like an angel.

Princess

You must think I'm very strange.

Hyacinth

Oh, no. I know another lady who does this sort of thing.

Princess

I wish I could make you trust me— I see you don't. You'd find I go pretty far—

Grandoni

She goes too far.

Princess

I'm not just some rich bitch amusing myself. I'm concerned—I'm convinced people of my class are living in a fool's paradise.

Grandoni

She wants to be part of the revolution—to guide it, to enlighten it.

Hyacinth

I'm sure she could manage it perfectly.

Princess

I've no such pretensions. Please don't laugh at me. What can be more absurd than for a woman with a title and great wealth to throw in her lot with the masses? You've a right to demand that I give all that up.

Hyacinth

But—

Princess

That I give all that up before you believe me. Well, I'm ready! That's the least difficulty. I'm here to learn, not to teach.

Hyacinth

I'm not asking you to give anything up. Why give it up? It might come in handy.

Princess

What's your occupation?

Hyacinth

I'm a bookbinder.

Princess

And your mysterious friend?

Hyacinth

A chemist

Princess (as if seeing visions of a bomb maker)

Ah! And what do you call home?

Hyacinth

Lomax Place in the north of London.

Princess

No—I don't think I've heard of it.

Hyacinth

It isn't much. I live with a dressmaker.

Princess

Do you mean——?

Grandoni

Is she your wife?

Hyacinth

No, no. She brought me up.

Princess

And your family?

Hyacinth

I have no family.

Princess

None at all?

Hyacinth (emphatically)

None at all!

Princess (seeing his annoyance)

Perhaps that's best— Do you think anything will occur soon?

Hyacinth

Pardon?

Princess

That there'll be a great crisis— That you'll make yourselves felt?

Grandoni

Please don't do anything for another hour or two. I want to enjoy the play.

Princess

You cannot answer, of course. But remember what I just said. I'll give up everything—everything.

(Sholto returns with Milly. The conversation continues for a few minutes in mime.)

Sholto

My dear fellow, you were born under a lucky star.

Hyacinth

I never suspected it!

Sholto

Why, what in the world to you want? You have the faculty, the precious faculty to inspire women with an interest—but an interest! Don't be afraid, you'll go far.

(The conversation lapses back into mime. Sholto leads off the Princess and Grandoni.)

Milly

She's a tidy lot, your Princess, by what I can learn.

Hyacinth

What do you know about her?

Milly

What that fellow told me.

Hyacinth

And, what was that?

Milly

Well, she's a bad 'un as ever was. Her own husband had to turn her out of the house.

Hyacinth

I could care less about that.

Milly

Don't you? Well, in that case, I do!

BLACKOUT

ACT II
Scene 5. A Room in Paul Muniment's House

Paul and Hyacinth are talking.

Hyacinth

She wants to see you; she asked me to bring you. She was very serious.

Paul

To bring me—bring me where? You talk as if I were a sample from your shop or a little dog you had for sale.

Hyacinth

Well, you're a friend of mine. That's enough for her.

Paul

You mean, I suppose, that it ought to be enough for me that she's a friend of yours?

Hyacinth

Certainly. I vouch for her.

Paul

Are you sure she isn't making game of you?

Hyacinth

I don't think so. What good would it do her?

Paul

That, I don't know. But she's one of them—and they're capable of anything.

Hyacinth

Be realistic. They're not all evil. People can't help it because they're born rich.

Paul

Undoubtedly, she's an idle, perhaps a profligate female.

Hyacinth

If you'd seen her, you wouldn't talk that way.

Paul

God forbid, I should see her then, if she's so charming. I don't need to be corrupted.

Hyacinth

And you think I'm in danger?

Paul (good-naturedly)

No—you're immune. You're already such a little mass of corruption.

Hyacinth

Leave off fooling. There are unselfish people—

Paul

I'm not in the least surprised that the aristocracy is curious to know what we're up to, and wants very much to look into it.

Hyacinth

Are you afraid I'll blab secrets to her?

Paul

What secrets could you tell her, my pretty lad?

Hyacinth (upset)

You don't trust me—you never have.

Paul

We will someday. Don't be afraid. And when we do, you'll be very disappointed.— Now tell me about this fellow Sholto—I haven't actually met him, though I've seen him at one of our meetings.

Hyacinth

Captain Sholto isn't the same sort as the Princess. Quite

different.

Paul

Different, of course. She's a handsome woman, and he's an ugly man. But, neither of them will save us or spoil us. Their curiosity is natural, but I've other things to do than to show them around,—or to be shown around by them. You can tell her Serene Highness that I'm much obliged.

Hyacinth

You show Lady Aurora around—what's the difference? If it's right for her to take an interest, why isn't it right for the Princess?

Paul

All I know of Lady Aurora is that she comes to sit with my sister. If the Princess will do as much, I'll see what I can do. But apart from that, I shall never take a grain of interest in her feelings for the masses.

Hyacinth

Do you think she can hurt me?

Paul

Yes, very likely. But you must hit her back, and really give it to her. That's your line, you know. I'm an ugly brute, but you're one of those taking little beggars that the women like— Only, you know, if she really hurt you, she'd have to deal with me.

Hyacinth

That's very kind of you to say, Paul.

Paul

We are friends, you know, for whatever that's worth. (going upstairs) Now, I've got to get Rosy ready before Lady Aurora comes or she'll be doing everything for her, and Rosy won't have that.

(Exit Paul. After a moment, enter Lady Aurora from the street door.)

Aurora

You never came to get the books!

Hyacinth

I didn't know we had an understanding I would.

Aurora

I've picked them out.

Hyacinth

That's awfully kind of you.

Aurora

Rosy will tell you where I live. She never forgets anything.

Hyacinth

She's a wonderful little witch. She terrifies me.

Aurora

Which do you think is the cleverer? Rosy or her brother?

Hyacinth

Oh, Paul will be Prime minister of England someday.

Aurora (pleased)

Do you believe that? I'm so glad.

Hyacinth

Why? You spend most of your time among the poor—and I'm sure you carry blessings with you— But for what? Wretched company we must be.

Aurora

I like it very much—you don't understand.

Hyacinth

Precisely. I don't understand. How can you surround yourself with squalor and disgusting company?

Aurora

Oh, I wish I could make you understand—

Hyacinth

Perhaps I do understand! Charity exists in your nature as a kind of passion.

Aurora

Yes, yes, it is a kind of passion. Whatever it is, it's my life. It's all I care for. When I was fifteen, I wanted to sell all I had to give to the poor. And ever since—I've wanted with all my heart to do something. It seemed as if my heart would break if I couldn't!

Hyacinth

I suppose you're very religious?

Aurora

I don't know. One has one's ideas. I think a great many clergymen do good, but there are others I don't like at all. I don't like society, and I don't think you would either if you saw much of it. At least the kind there is in London. But I've got out of it. I like Camberwell better. I'm a proper lunatic, you see. Well, I must go see Rosy.

(Aurora exits to Rosy's room.)

Hyacinth

I'll be in presently.

(There is a knock at the street door. Hyacinth goes to it and admits Madame Grandoni.)

Hyacinth

Madame Grandoni! What are you doing here?

Grandoni

I have come to see you. I went to your milliner's and she told me you were here.

Hyacinth

I'm honored. But, why have you come?

Grandoni

My dear young man, may I take the liberty of asking your age?

Hyacinth

Certainly; I'm twenty-four.

Grandoni

And, I hope you're industrious—and—what do they call it in England—steady?

Hyacinth

I don't think I'm very wild.

Grandoni

I don't know how one speaks in this country to young men like you. You are evidently intelligent and clever—and if you're disappointed, it will be a pity.

Hyacinth

Why should I be disappointed?

Grandoni

I dare say you expected great things from the Princess— You have been to her house. A mansion— You must tell me if I upset you. I'm very old fashioned.—I speak my mind.

Hyacinth

But, what is on it? I'm not easily upset. I only went to see her because she was kind enough to send for me.

Grandoni

You're not like the young men I have in mind. All the more reason. I came to warn you a little and I don't know how. If you were an Italian it would be different.

Hyacinth

How so? What do you want to warn me of?

Grandoni

Well—only to advise you a little. Don't give up anything.

Hyacinth (laughing)

What do I have to give up?

Grandoni

Don't give up yourself. There are things better even than being liked by a Princess, even a beautiful Princess. Hold fast to them.

Hyacinth

I think I understand you.

Grandoni

Before you go any farther, please think a little whether you are right.

Hyacinth

I'm not sure—

Grandoni

There are many people, these days, who think it useful to throw bombs into innocent crowds, and assassinate their own rulers—

Hyacinth

If I were to limit myself only to those means you approve of—?

Grandoni (very emphatically)

I don't approve of any means! I wish you well, young man. She wants you to come again. you will, I see that. Don't say I didn't warn you.

(Exit Madame Grandoni.)

Hyacinth

I—I'll remember.

(After a moment, Paul comes in.)

Paul

Rosy is making it pretty hot for me in there. So, I thought I'd escape.

(A knock at the street door. Paul goes and admits Poupin.)

Poupin

Forty thousand men are unemployed.

Paul

They say it's a bad year.

Poupin

They say that on purpose—to convey the impression that there are such things as good years. The good years are yet to come.

Paul

Hoffendahl's in London.

Poupin

Hoffendahl! That surprises me— Are you sure?

Paul

Quite sure.

Poupin

You have seen him?

Paul

Yes.

Hyacinth

What has he done?

Poupin

He's spent twelve years in a Prussian prison.

Hyacinth

What of that?

Paul

A man's foremost duty is not to get collared. If you want to prove you're capable, that's the way.

Poupin

Someone always gets caught.

Paul (to Hyacinth)

If they succeed in catching you, do as Hoffendahl has done. Suffer silently without betraying your friends. But, if they don't—make it your supreme duty—make it your religion to lie close—to keep yourself for another go.

Poupin

That's fearfully English.

Paul

No doubt, no doubt. You shall never share my fate—if I have a fate, and I can prevent your sharing it.

Hyacinth

What I want to know is, what's this Hoffendahl going to do for us?

Paul

That I don't know yet.

Poupin

What we need is a compact body in marching order.

Paul

I quite agree that the present state of things is infamous and hellish.

Hyacinth

I'm ready for anything.

Paul

Upon my life, I believe you're game. Would you like to see him—the real thing?

Hyacinth

The real thing?

Paul

A real revolutionary. You've never seen it, you only think you have.

Hyacinth

Why haven't you shown me before?

Poupin

You weren't ready.

BLACKOUT

ACT III
SCENE 6. A ROOM IN THE MANSION OF THE PRINCESS CASAMASSIMA

The Prince, an Italian nobleman, is talking to Madame Grandoni.

Prince (upset)

Never?

Grandoni

Surely, you know your wife as well as I do?

Prince

How can one know a woman like that? I hoped she'd see me five little minutes.

Grandoni

For what purpose?

Prince

To rest my eyes on her beautiful face.

Grandoni

Did you come to England for that?

Prince

For what else should I have come? She is killing me inch by inch.

Grandoni

She'd be much more likely to kill you if you were living with her.

Prince

She hasn't killed you.

Grandoni

Oh, me? I'm past killing. I'm hard as stone. Our troubles don't kill us—it's we who must kill them. I've buried not a few.

Prince (uninterested in her philosophy)

How does she look today?

Grandoni

As always. Like an angel— I'm very sorry for you, Prince.

Prince

I wanted to see myself how she's living.

Grandoni

That's very natural.

Prince

I've been hearing things, lots of things.

Grandoni

Lots of rubbish, no doubt.

Prince

She spends a great deal of money.

Grandoni

Indeed, she does. She thinks she's a model of thrift. If there's a virtue she prides herself on, it's her economy.

Prince

I wonder if she knows that I spend almost nothing at all. I'd rather live on bread and water than that she should fail to make a great appearance.

Grandoni

Her appearance is all that you could wish.

Prince

Why does this dreary country please her?

Grandoni

It's the common people.

Prince

That's what I've been hearing. Who was that man I met before?

Grandoni

The Princess's bookbinder.

Prince

Her bookbinder? You mean one of her lovers!

Grandoni

Prince, how can you ever dream she'll live with you again?

Prince

Why does she have him in her drawing room? Where were his books? His bindings?

Grandoni

I told you—she's making a study of the people. The young man you saw is a study—or part of it.

Prince

The more I know, the less I understand. Is it your idea that she's quite crazy? I don't care if she is.

Grandoni

We are all quite crazy, I think. But the Princess no more than the rest of us. She must try everything. At present she's trying democracy.

Prince

And what do people say?

Grandoni

Oh, a lady can do anything in this country.

Prince

There are things it's better to conceal.

Grandoni

I may as well give you the key to your wife's conduct: she's ashamed of having married you.

Prince

Ashamed! Ashamed to be a Princess of the House of Casamassima?

Grandoni

She considers that as the darkest hour of her life, she sold herself to you for a title and a fortune. No matter that she wanted it at the time. She will spend the rest of her life doing penance for that sin.

Prince

I know she pretends to have been forced— Well, if not the bookbinder, what about this English Captain?

Grandoni

This English Captain?

Prince

Godfred Gerald Sholto.

Grandoni

He's the last one you need worry about. He doesn't count the least bit.

Prince (dumbfounded)

Why doesn't he count?

Grandoni

Some people don't, you know. He knows better than to even think he does.

Grandoni

Why not, when she receives him always—lets him go wherever she goes?

Grandoni

He's a convenience—he works without wages.

Prince

Isn't he in love with her?

Grandoni

Of course. But he has no more hope than you do.

Prince

Ah, poor fellow.

Grandoni

He accepts the situation better than you do.

Prince

Because he is allowed to see her.

Grandoni

But she takes no notice of him.

Prince

I will go. But tell her I may come back.

Grandoni

It's utterly useless.

(The Prince bows to her very courteously and goes out. Grandoni walks around uneasily, then sinks into a chair. Enter Hyacinth with some books.)

Hyacinth

I'm afraid the books are very dusty.

Grandoni

The Princess will probably see you in a few hours.

Hyacinth

I really hope so.

Grandoni

People sometimes come and leave without seeing her. It all depends on her mood.

Hyacinth

Even after she has sent for them?

Grandoni

Who can tell whether she has sent for them or not?

Hyacinth

But, she sent for me.

Grandoni

Oh yes, she sent for you, poor young man. Sholto has come like that more than once, and gone away no better off.

Hyacinth

Captain Sholto?

Grandoni

She is a capriciossa.

Hyacinth

I don't understand the way you speak of her. You seem her friend, yet you say things that are not very favorable to her.

Grandoni

I say much worse to her than I ever permit myself to say to you. I'm rude, but I'm not treacherous. At any rate, you are here.

Hyacinth

Decidedly, I am here.

Grandoni

And, how long shall you stay? Pardon me if I ask. That's part of my rudeness.

Hyacinth

Till tomorrow morning. I must be at my work by noon.

Grandoni

That will do very well. You remember I told you to remain faithful?

Hyacinth

That was very good advice. But, I think you exaggerate my danger.

Grandoni

Impossible, I think. You're one of those types that ladies like. I can be sure of that, I like you myself. At my age, a hundred and twenty!— Be happy, make yourself comfortable; but go home tomorrow! Perhaps I shall go tomorrow.

Hyacinth

I have to work. That's reason enough for me.

Grandoni

Do you admire everything here? Does it give you pleasure?

Hyacinth

So much! I cannot tell you how much!

Grandoni

Poor boy.

(Enter the Princess.)

Princess (addressing herself immediately to Hyacinth)

Is it true that you've never seen a park or any of the beauties of nature?

Hyacinth

Perfectly true.

Princess

I'm so glad, I'm so glad. I've never been able to show anything new to anyone, especially to a fine, sensitive mind.— This place is tumbling to pieces. I don't want you to think I'm sunk in luxury and throw money away. Never! Never!

Hyacinth

You live according to your means. I would live like this if I could.

Princess

Would you? But, you must learn for yourself what it really is before we blow it up. You and I are the barbarians, you know.

Hyacinth

You certainly don't look that part.

Princess

Oh, I am whether I look it or not.

Hyacinth

The aristocracy isn't all that bad.

Princess

If we believe in the coming democracy—why not try to put its spirit in our lives? I try to do it in my relations with you—but you hang ridiculously back. You're really not a bit democratic.

Hyacinth

I've been cautioned against you.

Princess

I can very easily understand that— I've given no proofs as yet. Who was it that warned you against me?

Hyacinth

A friend of mine in London—Paul Muniment.

Princess

Paul Muniment?

Hyacinth

I mentioned him to you the first time we met. He's awfully wise.

Princess

What does he know about me?

Hyacinth

Nothing except what I've told him.

Princess

Well, you mustn't have given me a very good character.— I like his name, perhaps I should like him.

Hyacinth

You'd like him much better than you do me.

Princess

How do you know how much I like you or how little?— Never mind that, I like you a good deal. Now tell me what's going on among your friends. Is anything going to be done?— You think I'm a police spy, don't you?

Hyacinth

The idea never occurred to me.

Princess

It should—if you're going to be a conspirator.

Hyacinth

If you were in with the police, you wouldn't waste your time with me.

Princess

If would be my first care to make you think that. So much the better if you've no troublesome suspicions.

Hyacinth

There isn't much to tell. I've taken an oath to sacrifice myself, that's all.

Princess

To what?

Hyacinth

To whatever is asked. I gave my life away.

Princess

Be so good as to explain what you're talking about?

Hyacinth

I really do trust you, but I'll give you no names. There's no special reason to go into details. They wanted an obliging man— Well, the place was vacant, and I offered my services.

Princess (abstractedly)

I suppose you're right, we must pay for all we do. (after a moment) I think I know the person into whose power you've placed yourself.

Hyacinth

Possibly, but I doubt it.

Princess

You don't think I've gone that far? Why not?

Hyacinth

If you've gone that far, you've gone very far indeed.

Princess

Does he, by any chance, want an obliging young woman?

Hyacinth

I don't think he cares much for women.

Princess (lightly)

You've very nearly betrayed him to me. Have a care.

Hyacinth

I've seen the holy of holies. People go about thinking everything's fine and all's well with the world. But, there's an immense underground. The upper classes know nothing about it. A vast trap is being prepared.

Princess

And so you've put your head in a noose. (pause) YOUR MAN'S DIEDRICH HOFFENDAHL!

Hyacinth

Well, you really have gone further than I thought.

Princess

So! You've taken a vow of blind obedience.

Hyacinth

Yes.

Princess

To kill if necessary?

Hyacinth

Yes.

Princess

It's very serious, isn't it? Very serious, indeed.

Hyacinth

The serious part is yet to come. For now, I simply wait.

Princess

Perhaps nothing will happen.

Hyacinth

That would be very disappointing. But I have decided to live each day, each hour—as if it might be my last.

Princess

There will probably be a great many good days left.

Hyacinth

The more the better. Only, I no longer care for the things you care for.

Princess

What are you talking about? We both believe in the same thing.

Hyacinth

Do we? From the moment I pledged my life to the people, I ceased to give a damn about them!

Princess

You not longer care for the revolution?

Hyacinth

Not a damn!

Princess

You're very remarkable. You're splendid.

Hyacinth

I'd like to be.

Princess

Yes—I see that. You want to be one of them. Fancy the strange, the bitter fate: to be a perfect gentleman in gesture and feeling, and yet to look at the good things of life only through the glass of a pastry cook's window.

Hyacinth

Every class has its humble pleasures.

Princess

So your act is purely disinterested?

Hyacinth

I think it is correct to describe it that way.

Princess

That's wonderful, really. Only no one will believe it, you know.

Hyacinth

That doesn't matter to me. I'm glad YOU know. You're the only one I've spoken to.

Princess

I'm flattered. You must trust me a good deal.

Hyacinth

I told you I do.

Princess (suddenly)

I am going to introduce you to Lady Marchmont! Will you let me?

Hyacinth

Yes, of course, but—

Princess

Then come along. She's going to be here now.

Hyacinth

But, who is—

Princess

You'll see.

(Exit Princess and Hyacinth. After a moment Grandoni stirs in her chair where she has been dozing. Sholto enters.)

Grandoni

I'm glad to see you! What good wind has brought you here?

Sholto

Didn't you know I was coming?

Grandoni

I know nothing of the affairs of this house. I've given them up at last. I remain in my room, mostly. From the moment you come in it's a little better. But, it's very bad.

Sholto

What's bad?

Grandoni

Perhaps you'll be able to tell me where Christina is heading?

I've always been faithful to her. I've always been loyal. But today, I've lost my patience.

Sholto

I'm not sure what you're talking about, but if I understand you—I think it's magnificent.

Grandoni

You're worse than she is: you delight in all her antics because you're cynical. It passes all bounds. The scandal's too great.

Sholto

Dear Madame Grandoni, you cannot make it worse and you cannot make it better. Actually, no scandal can possibly attach itself to our friend.

Grandoni

What do you mean, when a lady has a bookbinder come live with her?

Sholto

It all depends who the lady is, and what she is.

Grandoni

She had better take care of one thing first—that she shall not have been separated from her husband—with a hundred stories!

Sholto

The Princess can carry off even that.

Grandoni

Who's to know he's her bookbinder? It's the last thing you'd take him for.

Sholto

She has chosen him carefully.

Grandoni

Carefully!

Sholto

It was I who chose him, dear lady.

Grandoni

It was a fine turn you did him, poor young man.

Sholto

Certainly, he'll be sacrificed. But haven't I been sacrificed?

Grandoni

I hope he bears it as well as you! It's too bad to spoil him for his station in life. How can he ever go back?

Sholto

Too bad! He's an abominable little conspirator with I don't know what bloody ideas. He gets what he deserves.

Grandoni

And, what does Christina deserve?

Sholto

Oh, lots of punishment. But it won't be the loss of reputation. She's too distinguished.

Grandoni

Why not?

Sholto

Because she has no regard for public opinion. Because she can do without it, it will never be taken from her.

Grandoni

At least you make another person in the house. So long as you are here, I won't go off.

Sholto

Depend upon it, I shall hang on tight, till I am turned off.

Grandoni

How can you stand it?

Sholto

I want to watch what becomes of the little beggar.

Grandoni

He's much too good for his fate. You're horrible.

Sholto

And pray, wasn't I too good for mine?

Grandoni (dryly)

By no means!

(Hyacinth enters and Grandoni retires to her chair.)

Sholto

Good morning, my dear fellow, I thought I should find you here.

Hyacinth

Who told you I was here?

Sholto

Why, I knew the Princess was capable of asking you, so—when I learned you were out of town, I concluded you must be here.

Hyacinth

I see. You're sure Millicent didn't tell you?

Sholto

Have you still got your back up a little?

Hyacinth

Not at all.

Sholto

You have no reason at all to be jealous.

Hyacinth

No.

Sholto

Just because you met her in the street after you met me in the same neighborhood is no reason to think she was coming to meet me.

Hyacinth

I agree perfectly.

(Pause.)

Sholto

How are you coming on? With the Princess, I mean.

Hyacinth

Very well, thank you.

Sholto

You understand my interest in you: I'm your sponsor. I put you forward.

Hyacinth

There are a great many things in the world I don't understand—but the thing I understand least is your interest in me. If I were you, I wouldn't give a damn for the sort of person I happen to be!

Sholto

That proves how different my nature is from yours! But, I don't believe it, my dear boy, you're too generous for that— It's very grand, her having brought you down here. I wanted to see it with my own eyes.

Hyacinth

Hardly surprising, considering I was put forward by you.

Sholto

It doesn't make any difference to her. It never signifies a lot to her what I may think. Look here, one good turn deserves another—get her to—put me forward, will you?

Hyacinth

I don't understand you. Surely you don't mean with Millicent?

Sholto (laughing amiably)

It isn't possible you're jealous? I don't mean Miss Henning.— The courage of it, the insolence of it, there isn't another woman in England who could carry it off.

Hyacinth

That's nothing. Just now she introduced me to Lady Marchmont.

Sholto

God, did she dare do that? I'd have given ten pounds just to see it. There's no one like her. Did you enjoy meeting the wife of our noble prime minister?

Hyacinth

Too much. Such excesses are dangerous. Well, I shall ask the Princess to keep you.

Sholto

Lucky little beggar, with your fireside talks! Where does she sit now in the evening? Never mind! I told you she's the cleverest woman in Europe. But there are some mysteries you can't see into unless you have a heart. Our Princess isn't troubled by that sort of thing. My only motive is to watch her, adore her, to see her lead her life, and act out her extraordinary nature. The rest's mere gabble.

Hyacinth

You don't care for the social question, then?

Sholto

I only took it up because she did. My dear Robinson, for me there's only one thing in life: to look at that woman when I can. Get her to keep me here.

Hyacinth

I'll use what influence I have, but—

Sholto

It would be an act of common humanity.

Hyacinth

You took up the social question because she did? But why did she take it up?

Sholto

You'll have to worm that out of her yourself.

Hyacinth

Do you mean the way she treats you proves she has no heart? What you said just now—

Sholto

I mean the way she treats you!

Hyacinth

You think I'm heading for a fall?

Sholto

Don't say I didn't warn you. The day I saw she was turning her attention to the rising democracy, I began to collect little democrats. That's how I collected you.

BLACKOUT

ACT III
Scene 7. The Same, a Few Days Later

Mr. Vetch has come to see Hyacinth on a matter of business.

Vetch

Dear Mr. Robinson, I'm so sorry for you. I wanted to write, but I promised Pinnie I wouldn't. It wouldn't have killed her if she had been like you or me. The doctor says she was impoverished—so weak and low she had nothing to go on.

Hyacinth

I don't know what to say to you. I can never blame you when you're so kind, but I wish to God I had known. Don't you think you might have written me a word?

Vetch

No responsibility in my life has ever distressed me more. There were obvious reasons for calling you back, but Pinnie insisted that you must finish your visit. It was very difficult.

Hyacinth

I can imagine nothing more simple. When your nearest and

dearest are dying, you're usually sent for.

Vetch

My dear boy, this case was exceptional. Your visit to the Princess Casamassima had an aura of importance.

Hyacinth

It's not important at all.

Vetch

Pinnie made a tremendous point of your not being disturbed. If she had been dying in a corner like a starved cat, she would have faced her fate alone, rather than cut short your visit by a single hour.

Hyacinth

She spun her ideas—she always did—out of nothing.

Vetch

She had made up her mind that you had formed a connection by means of which someday, by some means, you will eventually come into your own— We had to leave her that idea.

Hyacinth

Yes, of course. I'm glad I furnished Pinnie such entertaining ideas.

Vetch

Is she really a Princess?

Hyacinth (absently)

What? Yes, of course.

Vetch

If I can help you in any way, you must lean on me.

Hyacinth

That's just what I was going to say to you.

Vetch

Have you been making love to this Princess?

Hyacinth

It's not that way.

Vetch

Has she been making love to you then?

Hyacinth

If you saw her, you wouldn't think that—

Vetch

How shall I ever see her?

Hyacinth

It's not impossible. If you like, I shall introduce you now. (Vetch shakes his head sadly) She wants to meet all my friends in the

Place. She'd be very interested in you because of your opinions.

Vetch

Ah, I've no opinions now. I only had them to frighten Pinnie.

Hyacinth (wryly)

She was easily frightened.

Vetch

And easily reassured. But, take care this great lady doesn't lead you too far.

Hyacinth

How do you mean?

Vetch

Isn't she a conspirator? A dabbler in plots and treasons?

Hyacinth

You should see this place. You should see what she wears—

Vetch

You mean she's inconsistent? My dear boy, she'd be a strange woman if she wasn't. Pinnie left you some money. She had insurance, would you believe it? Twenty pounds.

Hyacinth

Well, for me that's a small fortune. Too bad she didn't have the use of it.

Vetch

She had hoped you'd go abroad and see the world. She had a particular wish you'd go to Paris.

Hyacinth

Ah, Paris!

Vetch

She would have liked you to take a little run down to Italy.

Hyacinth

Doubtless that would be very jolly. But there's a limit to what twenty pounds can buy.

Vetch

I propose to add my savings.

Hyacinth

That's very kind, but you're getting along and may need it.

Vetch

My dear boy, I shall look to you to be the support of my old age.

Hyacinth

You may do so with perfect confidence, so far as it lies within my power. But there is the danger you mentioned earlier. The trifling problem of my being imprisoned or hanged.

Vetch

It's precisely because I think the danger will be less if you go abroad, that I urge you most passionately to take the chance.

Hyacinth

It is certainly a temptation. Something I should very much like to do.

Vetch

I believe it was Pinnie's dearest wish. Do it for her.

Hyacinth

I will give it careful consideration. But I have obligations—

Vetch

I am sure, I am sure.

(Hyacinth and Vetch embrace, and Hyacinth exits. Vetch shakes his head sadly and is about to leave when Madame Grandoni appears.)

Grandoni

Mr. Vetch! Please do not go away, the Princess Casamassima has learned you are here and wishes to speak to you. She had received your note.

(Exit Grandoni and enter Princess.)

Princess

I know who you are, I know who you are.

Vetch

I wonder if you also know what I would like to speak to you about?

Princess

No, but it doesn't matter, I am very glad. You must know how much interest I take in your nephew.

Vetch

It's for his sake I ventured—

Princess

I hope you won't ask me to give him up?

Vetch

On the contrary, on the contrary—

Princess

Surely he doesn't think I shall cease to be his friend?

Vetch (very excited)

I don't know what he thinks, I don't know what he hopes. Properly speaking, it's no business of mine. I'm not really a blood relation. I thank you for your great kindness to him.

Princess (considering)

All the same, I don't think you like it.

Vetch

He has told me very little about you. He doesn't know I have taken this step.

Princess

Step? That's what people say when they're doing something disagreeable.

Vetch

I seldom call on ladies. Now that I see you, now that I hear you, I begin to understand. Is there any chance that Hyacinth will return while I am here?

Princess

I have given Madame Grandoni instructions to occupy him until you are safely away.

Vetch

Please don't tell him we have met.

Princess

I won't, but he'll guess it. He's incredibly intuitive.

Vetch

How well you know him.

Princess

I'm extremely curious as to what you have to say to me. I remember about you now. You were a great democrat in the old days, but of late, you've ceased to care about the people.

Vetch

I see you think I'm a renegade. (excitedly) What I want is this—that you'll—that you'll—

Princess

That I will——?

Vetch

Princess, I'd give my own life for that boy— You've taken possession of his life.

Princess

Yes. But as I understand you, you don't complain of it! I know the terrible story of his mother.

Vetch

It was my fault he ever heard of it. I thought it would do him good. I don't know what was in my head. I wanted him to quarrel with society. Now I want him reconciled to it.

Princess

Ah, but he is! He's a perfect little aristocrat.

Vetch

Those are not the opinions he expresses to me. He said only the other day that he would regard himself as the most contemptible of human beings if he did nothing.

Princess

I assure you the misery of the people is by no means always on his mind. He thinks civilization will be sacrificed utterly if the ignorant masses get the upper hand.

Vetch

He needn't be afraid. That will never happen.

Princess

We can at least try.

Vetch (passionately)

Try what you like, Madame, but for God's sake, get the boy out of this! The world's very sad and hideous, and I am happy to say that I shall soon have done with it. But before I go, I want to save the child! If he doesn't believe in it, what's he in it for, Madame? What devilish folly has he undertaken?

Princess (after a pause)

He's a strange mixture of contradictory impulses. How can I go into his affairs with you? How can I tell you his secrets. I don't know them, and if I did—well, fancy me!

Vetch

Why do you take such a line? Why do you believe such things?

Princess

My dear sir, how do you know what I believe? You think me affected, but I'm only trying to be natural. And you? Are you not yourself a little contradictory? You don't want our young friend to pry into the misery of the people—because it excites his sense of justice—

Vetch

I don't care a fig for his sense of justice—or the misery of the people. I only want to help him, to get him free.

Princess

Don't misrepresent him. He's one of the most civilized men in the world.

Vetch

I don't understand you. If you like him because he's one of the lower orders, how can you like him because he's a civilized little aristocrat?

Princess

Dear Mr. Vetch, I'm not bound to explain myself to you. Nothing is more annoying than to have one's sincerity questioned. Let us say, he has his charms— Come, pull yourself together. We both take an interest in him, and I can't see why we should quarrel about him.

Vetch

God knows, I don't want to quarrel. I only want to get Hyacinth free.

Princess

Free from what?

Vetch

From some abominable secret brotherhood, some league of assassins that he belongs to—the thought of which keeps me awake at night. He's just the sort of impressionable youngster to be made a cat's-paw.

Princess

What grounds have you for believing this?

Vetch (a little more calmly)

Well, a great many; none of them very definite. His appearance, his manner— Dear lady, one feels those things, one guesses. I've appealed to the Poupins, and they assure me that he's as dear to them as their own child. That doesn't comfort me much for the simple reason that the old woman would be delighted to see her own son a martyr of the revolution. It may all be rubbish—but it's dangerous rubbish.

Princess

Don't speak to me of the French; I've never cared for them.

Vetch

That's awkward if you're a social revolutionary. You're likely to meet them.

Princess

Why do you call me a socialist? I hate cheap labels. What is it you suspect—for you must suspect something?

Vetch

Well, that he may have drawn some accursed lot to do some idiotic thing—something in which he doesn't believe.

Princess

If he doesn't believe in it, he can easily let it alone.

Vetch

Do you think he's a type to back out of his word?

Princess

One can never judge people in that way until they're tested. Haven't you ever taken the trouble to ask him?

Vetch

What would be the use? He'd tell me nothing.

Princess

I still don't see exactly how I am to help you.

Vetch

Do you want him to commit some atrocity?

Princess

Certainly not. Trust me and trust him, too. He's a gentleman and will behave as a gentleman.

Vetch

That's exactly what I'm afraid of.

Princess

Leave him to me—

Vetch

I've supposed for a long time that it was you or his chemist friend who got him into this scrape. It was you I suspected most—but if it isn't you, then—

Princess

I begin to lose patience with you! You had better go to him then!

Vetch

Of course, I'll go to him. I scarcely know him, but I'll speak my mind.

Princess

Better not! Leave him quiet. Leave him to me.

Vetch

Why not, why not? Doesn't he know?

Princess

No, he doesn't know; he has nothing to do with it. You'll spoil everything. Leave Paul Muniment to me. Leave him to me.

Vetch (going)

I beg you, I beg you.

Princess

Rest assured, I will not let our friend come to any harm if I can help it.

Vetch

Thank you,—thank you very much. (bowing, he goes out)

(The Princess stands lost in thought for a few moments. Grandoni comes in.)

Grandoni

Mr. Muniment.

(Exit Grandoni. Enter Paul.)

Princess

So, you've come! I didn't have to repeat my invitation.

Paul

It wouldn't have done you any good if you had.

Princess

My silence wasn't accidental.

Paul

I've only come now because my sister has hammered it at me that I ought to. I've been under the lash! If she had left me alone, I shouldn't have come.

Princess

You practice a racy sort of frankness. I'm not used to failing when it comes to men.

Paul

Naturally, the awkward things I say amuse you.

Princess

Not at all! You simply are different—although I expected you to be like this. I know you a good deal already.

Paul

From Robinson, I suppose.

Princess

More particularly from Lady Aurora.

Paul

Oh, she doesn't know much about me.

Princess

More than you think I fancy. She likes you.

Paul

Yes, she likes me.

Princess

And, I hope you like her.

Paul

Aye, she's a dear old girl.

Princess

I don't know that there's anyone I envy so much. She's got out of herself better than anyone I've ever known. She's submerged herself in the passion of helping others. That's why I envy her.

Paul (dryly)

It's an amusement like any other.

Princess

Don't belittle her. She has made a great many people less wretched!

Paul

How many, eh?

Princess

Well, one who's very near and dear to you.

Paul

Rosy makes Lady Aurora considerably less wretched!

Princess

Very likely, of course, as she does me.

Paul

What are you wretched about?

Princess

Why nothing at all, and everything! Still, I've been able to do some good.

Paul

For the poor, you mean?

Princess

Not yet. It's the convictions I've come to.

Paul

Convictions are a sort of innocent pleasure.

Princess

Having convictions is nothing. It's acting on them.

Paul

Doubtless.

Princess

It's far better, of course, when one's a man.

Paul

Women do pretty well what they like. My sister and you have managed between you to bring me to this.

Princess

More your sister than I. But why are you so reluctant to come?

Paul

Because I don't know what to make of you.

Princess

Most people don't. But why not come see for yourself?

Paul

And, being a prudent man, I hesitate to venture—

Princess

You consider very carefully what you attempt?

Paul

That I do—I do.

Princess

To do anything in association with you would be very safe—it would be sure to succeed.

Paul

That's what Robinson thinks. Poor fellow.

Princess

I care for him very much.

Paul

He's a sweet little lad, and putting Lady Aurora aside, he's quite the light of our little home.

Princess

Wouldn't someone else do his work quite as well?

Paul

I'm told he's a master hand.

Princess

I don't mean his bookbinding.

Paul

Ah, that work.

Princess

Let me do it. I want to do something for the cause you represent. Try me, try me. I'm not trifling. No, I'm not trifling.

Paul

I was afraid you'd be like this.

Princess

Like what?

Paul

Very persuasive. Very convincing. I've always had a fear of clever women.

Princess

You're the sort of man who ought to know how to use them.

Paul

I ought to—you're right.

Princess

I should like to do it in his place—that's what I should like.

Paul

You've got a lovely home.

Princess

Lovely? My dear, it's hideous.

Paul

Well, I like it.

Princess

You should have seen me before.

Paul

I wish I had. I like solid wealth.

Princess

You're as bad as Hyacinth. I'm the only consistent one.

Paul

I'd give my nose for such a place as this. You're not reduced to poverty.

Princess

I've a little left.

Paul

I'd lay a wager you've a great deal.

Princess

I could get money—I could get money.

Paul (going)

I don't trust women—I don't trust clever women.

Princess

Will you come back?

Paul

Yes, I'll come back.

(Exit Paul. After a moment, enter Grandoni.)

Grandoni

And, who may that be? Isn't that a new face?

Princess

He's a brother of the little person I took you to see— The chattering cripple with the wonderful manners.

Grandoni

Ah, she had a brother! So that was why you went.

Princess

There could have been no question of our seeing him. He was at his work.

Grandoni

And, is he to be the successor?

Princess

The successor?

Grandoni

To the little bookbinder?

Princess

What an absurd question!

(The Princess goes out angrily. Grandoni sinks into a chair and begins to knit. The Prince enters.)

Prince

What a black little hole it is. My wife should live here.

Grandoni

My dear friend, for all she's your wife—

Prince

It's true—it's true! She has lovers! I've seen it with my own eyes and I've come here to know!

Grandoni

Coming here won't help you much. If you're seen, you know for yourself.

Prince

You're afraid! You're afraid!

Grandoni

Sit down and be quiet, very quiet. I've ceased to pay attention.

Prince

Do you know she's gone to a house in a horrible quarter?

Grandoni

I think it highly probably, dear Prince.

Prince

And who is he? What does she want there? That's what I want to discover.

Grandoni

I haven't seen him—how can I tell you?

Prince

Is that kind to me—when I've counted on you?

Grandoni

I'm not kind any more, I'm angry.

Prince

Then, why don't you watch her, eh?

Grandoni

It's not her I'm angry with, it's myself.

Prince (puzzled)

For what?

Grandoni

For staying in this house.

Prince

What a house for a Princess! She might, at least, live in a manner befitting her.

Grandoni

The last time you thought it too expensive.

Prince

Is it because things are so bad you must go? He was in the house for over an hour. I saw him come. I saw him go. Who is he? This new one?

Grandoni

Was it for this you came to London? You had better go back to Rome.

Prince

Of course, I'll go back. But only if you tell me who this one is! How can you be so ignorant, dear friend, when he comes freely in and out of this place?

Grandoni

I sit in my room almost always now. I only come down to eat.

Prince

Better if you sat here. You could at least answer my questions.

Grandoni

I haven't the least desire to answer them. You must remember that I'm not here as your spy— He's a chemist's assistant.

Prince

A chemist's assistant. And the other one is a bookbinder.

Grandoni

Oh, him— You must wait till I'm free.

Prince

Free?

Grandoni

I must choose. I must hold my tongue if I stay. If I go away, I can tell you what I've seen—and plenty there is I've seen—more than I ever expected to.

Prince

Dearest friend, tell me this. Where does she go? For the love of

God, what is that house?

Grandoni

I know nothing of their houses.

Prince

Then, there are others? There are many?

Grandoni

There's a conspiracy.

Prince

You mean she's joined a secret society? Anarchists? But, perhaps, they only pretend?

Grandoni

Pretend? That's not Christina's way! She has gone to those houses to break up society. She's very much entangled. She has relations with people who are watched by the police.

Prince

And, is she watched by the police?

Grandoni

It's very possible.

Prince

Will she bring us to that scandal?

Grandoni

There's a chance she may get tired of it. Only the scandal may come before that.

Prince

She shall not break up society!

Grandoni

No, she'll bore herself to death before the coup is ripe. Give her time—give her time.

Prince

Give her time to muddy my name—

Grandoni

You can say nothing that I haven't said to her.

Prince

And how does she defend herself?

Grandoni

Defend herself? Did Christina ever do that! The only thing she says to me is: Don't be afraid. I promise you, by all that's sacred, you personally shan't suffer— She speaks as if she had the power. That's all very well. No doubt I'm a selfish old pig, but after all one has a heart for others, too—

Prince

And so have I. Give her time—it's certain she'll take it whether I give it or no. But I can, at least, stop giving her money.

Grandoni

She says you don't give her much.

Prince

It's enough to make all these scoundrels flock around her.

Grandoni

They're not scoundrels. That's the tiresome part of it.

Prince

Does this chemist take her money?

Grandoni

Perhaps—

Prince

Gigolo of revolution! And the famous Captain Sholto?

Grandoni

I haven't seen him for some time.

Prince

He doesn't like chemists and bookbinders?

Grandoni

It was he who first brought the bookbinder here—to please your wife.

Prince

And they've turned him out. Now, if only someone could turn them out.

Grandoni

Very true.

Prince

And the bookbinder. Is he still proposed for our admiration, or has he paid the penalties of his crimes?

Grandoni

His star is on the wane.

Prince

Poor fellow! Is the chemist his successor?

Grandoni

In some manner, I think so—

(Enter Hyacinth.)

Hyacinth

Excuse me, I wasn't aware you had company.

Grandoni

My visitor's going—but, I'm going, too. I'm all upset, therefore, kindly excuse me.

Prince

One moment, one moment. Please introduce me to the gentleman.

Grandoni (indicating the Prince to Hyacinth)

Prince Casamassima. He knows who you are.— If you talk long, she may come back.

(Exit Grandoni.)

Prince

Will you permit me to keep you one little minute? With Madame Grandoni I spoke of you. She told me you've changed your opinions. You desire no more the assassination of the rich?

Hyacinth

I've never desired any such thing!

Prince

Ah, no doubt I was mistaken. But today, you think we must have patience? That's also my view.

Hyacinth

Oh yes, we must have patience.

Prince

If I'm not mistaken, you know very well the Princess.

Hyacinth

She's been very kind to me.

Prince

She's my wife—perhaps you know—

Hyacinth

Yes.

Prince

Of course, you think it strange, my conversation. I want you—I want you to tell me something. To what house has she gone? Will you tell me that? She has gone to a house where they conspire—where they prepare horrible acts. Does she go only for the revolution—or does she go to be alone with him?

Hyacinth

With him?

Prince

With this chemist friend of yours?

Hyacinth

With him? I know nothing of the matter. (hastily) And, I don't care.

Prince

Then it's not true that you hate those abominations?

Hyacinth

Oh yes, I hate those abominations.

Prince

I hoped you would help me.

Hyacinth

When we're in trouble, we can't help each other much.

BLACKOUT

ACT IV
Scene 8. Rosy's Bedroom

The Princess has paid a visit and is about to leave. Paul is present. Hyacinth enters and is seen by the Princess.

Princess (noticing Hyacinth)

I'm very glad of your return.

Hyacinth (a little taken aback)

Well, how did you come here?

Princess

Oh, I get about. Captain Sholto brought me a week ago. I took the liberty of coming again, by myself today—because I wanted to see the whole family. (to Paul, with a hard note) When I come to see gentlemen, I like to find them.

Hyacinth

I was disappointed when I called at your house in South Street.

Princess

Oh, I've given up that house, and taken a quite different one.

(If Hyacinth expects to learn where the house is, he's to be disappointed, for the Princess does not tell him.)

Hyacinth

Is Madame Grandoni still at her post? You ought to bring her to see Rosy.

Rosy

I'm sure I'd be most happy to receive any friend of the Princess Casamassima.

Princess

I'd be happy to bring her—but she left.

Hyacinth

She left?

Princess

Yes, two days ago.

Hyacinth

It's too bad. I should like to have said goodbye to her.

Princess

You may imagine how I feel it.

Hyacinth

You mean the eyes of the world—

Princess

She couldn't put up with me any more. I'm too much of a scandal.

Hyacinth

What will she do?

Princess

I suppose she'll go and live with my husband. Funny, isn't it, that it should always be one of us—and that it matters so little which?

Hyacinth

She kept threatening a long time.

Princess

Oh, yes.

Paul (trying to break the tension)

You ought to tell us about foreign parts and the grand things you've seen. Except that our distinguished visitor must know all about them. (to Princess) Surely, you've seen nothing more worthy of your respect than Camberwell?

Princess

Is this the worst part?

Paul

The worst, Madame? What grand ideas you must have! We

admire Camberwell immensely.

Rosy

It's my brother's ideas that are grand. He wants everything changed. As if dirty people won't always make everything dirty. If everyone were clean, where would be the merit? You'd get no merit for keeping yourself tidy. Still, if it's a question of soap, everyone can begin with himself. My brother thinks the whole world ought to be as handsome as Brompton.

Princess

That's where all the artists and literary people live, isn't it?

Paul

Oh, I like Camberwell better than that.

Princess

I don't care about the artists.

Paul

Not when they've painted you such beautiful pictures? We know all about them—Mr. Robinson has told us all about your precious possessions.

Rosy

Was it all make-believe?

Princess

I've nothing in the world but the clothes on my back!

Hyacinth

I meant the things in the house.

Princess

There are no things in my house now.

Rosy

I shouldn't like that. Everything here belongs to me.

Princess

That's nice, of course, but—

Rosy

Do you think it's not right to have a lot of things about?

Princess

One must settle that for oneself. I don't like to be surrounded by things I don't care for. When thousands have no bread to put in their mouths, I can dispense with tapestry and old china.

Rosy

But, don't you think we ought to make the world more beautiful?

Princess

The world can wait to become beautiful until it becomes good enough. Is there anything so ugly as unjust privileges? When we want to beautify, we must begin at the right end.

Rosy

Surely, there are none of us, but what have our privileges. What do you say to mine: entertaining a Princess? If everyone was equal, where would be the gratification I feel in getting a visit from a grandee? No, no—no equality while I'm about.

(Enter Lady Aurora.)

Aurora (to Princess)

I'm so glad you waited. I was late.

Princess

Lady Aurora has graciously offered to take me to some of the other families she visits.

Aurora

Can you go now? We'll be late.

Princess

Yes, of course.

(The Princess and Lady Aurora exit.)

Rosy

Lady Aurora and the Princess seem to have become good friends.

Paul

What in the mischief does she want of her?

Hyacinth

What do you mean?

Paul

What does the beauty of beauties want of our poor plain lady? She has a totally different stamp. I don't know much about women, but I can see that.

Rosy

They both have the stamp of their rank.

Hyacinth

Who can tell what women want at any time?

Paul

Trouble with Millicent? Well, my boy, if you don't know more than that, you disappoint me. Perhaps, if we wait long enough she'll tell us.

Hyacinth

About Lady Aurora?

Paul

I don't mind about Lady Aurora so much; but what in the name of long journeys does she want with her?

Rosy

Don't you think you're worth a long journey? I'd go from one end of England to the other to make your acquaintance. He's in love with the Princess and he asks those senseless questions to cover it up.

Hyacinth

Are you sweet on her?

Paul

Sweet on her, sweet on her, my boy! I might just as well be sweet on the Dome of Saint Paul's.

Rosy

The Dome on Saint Paul's doesn't come to see you, and ask you to return the visit.

Paul

I don't return visits. I don't put myself out for the Princess. Isn't that sufficient answer to your accusations?

Hyacinth

I'm not sure. Your hanging off is more suspicious. It may mean you don't trust yourself, that you're afraid.

Paul

I should think my making up to her would suit your book.

Hyacinth

Do you suppose I'm afraid of you? Besides, why should I care now?

Rosy

What do you mean by that?

Paul (quickly)

He's just being mysterious. Pay no attention to him.

(Paul and Hyacinth come forward away from Rosy and talk low.)

Hyacinth

I didn't want to make a scene—but how will you like it when I'm strung up on the gallows?

Paul

You mean Hoffendahl's job?

Hyacinth

I didn't mean to speak of it, especially in front of Rosy, but it naturally came to my mind. I've been thinking about it a good deal.

Paul

What good does that do? You don't like it. Do you want to give it up?

Hyacinth

Not in the least. But, did you suppose I liked it?

Paul

My dear fellow, how could I tell? You like a lot of things I don't. You like excitement and emotions—whereas I go in for holy calm—for sweet repose.

Hyacinth

If you prefer calm, why do you associate yourself with a terrorist organization?

Paul (chuckling)

Isn't our movement as quiet as the grave?

Hyacinth

I see. You take only the quiet parts.

Paul

I'm as likely to be beside you on the gallows for all that. Look, there's one thing to remember—Hoffendahl may choose never to call on you.

Hyacinth

Somehow, I don't fancy either you or he get mixed up in things that don't come off.

Paul

There are three or four definite chances in your favor.

Hyacinth

I don't want second rate comfort.

Paul

What the devil do you want?

Hyacinth

Oh, to know how you feel about it—exactly what good you think it will do?

Paul

The execution, eh? Well, putting it at its worst, possibly none at all. It's intended as a warning, an admonishment.

Hyacinth

An admonishment!

Paul

They must learn they can't get away with it without paying a price.

Hyacinth

But, why strike at individuals?

Paul

Because we cannot effectively strike at the whole system—much as we would prefer to. There's no Bastille to storm—and if there were, we haven't the wherewithal to storm it. So we must be content with small, symbolic acts.

Hyacinth

I should rather storm the Bastille.

Paul

Amen. But that was in the days before machine guns were invented.

Rosy

Will you two stop conspiring and pay some attention to me? I really am getting annoyed.

BLACKOUT

ACT IV

Scene 9. Millicent's Shabby but Genteel Apartment

Millicent is putting on her gloves preparatory to going out. She goes to the door and steps back startled, admitting Hyacinth.

Milly

Whatever are you prowling about here for? You're up to no good, I'll be bound.

Hyacinth

Sorry if I frightened you. I was about to knock.

Milly

That's all right. Gave me a start.

Hyacinth

Where were you going so fast? What are you doing?

Milly

Well, I never did see such a manner—from one that knocks about like you! I'm going to see a friend. Have you anything to say to that?

Hyacinth (archly)

On what errand of mercy, on what secret mission?

Milly

Secret yourself! Why aren't you with your Princess instead of spying on me?

Hyacinth

Are you playing me false, Miss Henning?

Milly

False, false! You're a pretty one to talk of falsity when a woman has only to leer at you from an opera box—

Hyacinth

Don't say anything about her!

Milly

And pray, why not about her, I should like to know? You don't pretend she's a decent woman, I suppose.

Hyacinth

You're not really jealous of anyone. You pretend that only to throw dust in my eyes.

Milly

If you've come to see me, only to make low jokes at my expense, you had better have stayed away altogether. In the first place, it's rude, in the second place, it's silly, and in the third place, I see through you.

Hyacinth

My dear Milly, the motions you go through, the resentment you profess, are all a kicking up of dust which I blow away with a breath. (gesturing as puffing away a cloud of smoke) But go on, say anything you like.

Milly

The first thing I require of any friend is that he should respect me. You had a bad life, I know what to think about that.

Hyacinth

It's good to be with you. You understand everything.

Milly

I understand everything you like. You little rascal—has your Princess given you the sack?

Hyacinth

It may well be.

Milly

I'm glad you admit that!

Hyacinth

I'm a bigger Philistine than you, Miss Henning.

Milly

I don't believe you know, with all your thinking, what you do think.

Hyacinth

It's astonishing how you sometimes put your finger on things. I intend to think no more. I mean to give it up. Let us live in the present hour.

Milly

I don't care how I live, nor where I live, so long as I can do as I like. You were never satisfactory to me as a friend—and I consider myself remarkably good natured to have kept you so little up to the mark. You never tell me anything!

Hyacinth

What is it you want me to tell you, dear child? I'll tell you anything in life you like.

Milly

You'll tell me no end of rot. Certainly, I tried kindness on you.

Hyacinth (good-naturedly)

Try it again. Don't give up.

Milly

Well then, has she chucked you?

(Hyacinth turns away.)

Milly

THE BITCH!

Hyacinth

Milly, you're a sweetheart!

Milly

Why didn't you say so right away? I wouldn't have been so rough with you.

Hyacinth

This isn't rough.

Milly (holding him)

You're trembling.

Hyacinth

Very likely. I'm a nervous wreck, you know.

Milly

You need sympathy.

Hyacinth

A tablespoon twice a day.

Milly

I like you now.

Hyacinth

It's a pity I've always been so terribly under the influence of women. The sex in general has been very nice to me.

Milly

Does she know—your trumpery Princess?

Hyacinth

About my vow? Yes—but she doesn't mind.

Milly

That's most uncommonly kind of her.

Hyacinth

You know nothing about her.

Milly

How do you know what I know, please? Hasn't she treated you most shamelessly—and you a reg'lar dear?

Hyacinth

Not in the least. My opinions have changed and hers haven't—that's all.

Milly

And your grand lady still goes in for costermongers?

Hyacinth

Something has to be done and she wants to do it. I have too many scruples.

Milly

If she hasn't kicked you out, why do you say she has?

Hyacinth

I don't know; I can't make it out. Something has happened, but I don't know what it is.

Milly

Well, I can make it out! You silly baby, has Paul been making up to her Serene Highness? Is that his game? Do you mean to say she'd look at the likes of him?

Hyacinth

Paul! He's as fine a man as any born. They've the same views. They're doing the same work.

Milly

And probably sleeping in the same bed! It makes WORK easier.

Hyacinth (protesting)

That's enough, Milly, I won't have you—

Milly

So, he hasn't changed his opinions, then—not like you?

Hyacinth

No, he knows what he wants, he knows what he thinks.

Milly

Oh, I dare say. Don't be a saint, they're a precious pain.

Hyacinth

A man shouldn't turn on his friends.

Milly

Or betray him with his woman. You need someone to fight for you!

Hyacinth

My dear girl, you're a comfort.

(There is a knock at the door. Milly looks uncomfortable, but straightening her shoulders, goes to the door.)

Hyacinth

You know, you still haven't told me where you were going?

(Milly opens the door and admits Captain Sholto who is armed with a large bouquet of flowers.)

Sholto

My dear Miss Henning, when you were late—ah, my dear Robinson, I haven't seen you in some time, delighted.

Hyacinth (perceiving the situation immediately, turns on his heel and walks out)

I was just leaving.

Sholto

But, do stay, my dear fellow. Has there been some quarrel? Allow me to be the peacemaker.

BLACKOUT

ACT IV

Scene 10. Hyacinth's Workroom

Late at night. Vetch is dozing in his chair, his violin at his side. Hyacinth enters.

Vetch

Oh, I didn't hear you. You're very quiet.

Hyacinth

You've been asleep.

Vetch

No, I've not been asleep. I don't sleep much these days.

Hyacinth

Then, you're meditating.

Vetch

Yes, I've been thinking. I'm glad to see you. I've been looking at your books. You do fine work—you're a master. With such a hand you'll make a fortune and become famous.

Hyacinth

How many bookbinders have ever become famous?

Vetch

Well—

Hyacinth

My dear old friend, you've something on your mind.

Vetch

You read my thoughts. I've forced myself to let you alone.

Hyacinth

You had better let me come live with you as I suggested after Pinnie's death.

Vetch

Will you, my boy? Will you come tonight?

Hyacinth

Tonight?

Vetch

Tonight has worried me more than any other. I got to thinking of Pinnie. If I believed in ghosts, I should believe I had seen her. Then, I could bear it no longer, and I came here.

Hyacinth

Why don't you spend the night on my bed? I'll sleep on the floor.

Vetch

No, no.

Hyacinth

It won't be any different in your room.

Vetch

I'll get another room.

Hyacinth

At this time of night? Your reason totters on its throne.

Vetch

Very good. We'll get a room tomorrow.

Hyacinth

But, I have to give a month's notice here.

Vetch

Ah, you're backing out!

Hyacinth

Pinnie wouldn't have said that. She'd have believed me.

Vetch

If you'll make me a promise, I'll believe that.

Hyacinth

Any promise you like.

Vetch

Oh, that isn't what I want. Make me a promise that you'll never, under any circumstances, "do" anything.

Hyacinth

What do you mean?

Vetch

Anything those people expect of you.

Hyacinth

Those people?

Vetch

Don't torment me by pretending not to understand: you know the people I mean. I can't call them by their names, because I don't know who they are. But you do—and they know you.

Hyacinth

I suppose I know the people you've in mind. But, I don't grasp the need for these solemnities.

Vetch

Don't they want to make use of you?

Hyacinth

I see what you mean: you think they want me to blow up some train for them. Well, if that's what troubles you, you may sleep sound. I shall never do any of their work.

Vetch

Do you take your oath to that? Never anything?

Hyacinth

Never anything at all.

Vetch

Will you swear it on Pinnie's memory?

Hyacinth

Willingly.

Vetch

Then, you are saved!

Hyacinth

No, I'm damned.

BLACKOUT

ACT V

SCENE 11. THE PRINCESS'S HOUSE

The Princess is pacing, dressed to go out. Paul enters.

Princess

You're braver than I gave you credit for.

Paul

I shall have to be brave if I associate a while longer with you.

Princess

I didn't expect you.

Paul

Well, here I am—that's the great thing.

Princess

It will be a still greater thing when you're there.

Paul

Where is it? I don't think you told me.

(The Princess gives him a letter which he reads, then crushes and throws in the fire.)

Princess

What are you afraid of? I take it the house is known to the police. If we go, I suppose we must admit that we go.

Paul

No writing—no writing.

Princess

You're terribly careful.

Paul

Careful of you—yes.

Princess

This gives me a much less keen emotion than when I act by myself.

Paul (hesitating)

Is that what you go in for—keen emotion?

Princess

Surely, don't you?

Paul

God forbid! I hope to have as little of any sort as possible.

Princess

It would be hard if one couldn't have a little pleasure on the way.

Paul

My pleasure is keeping very cool.

Princess

I like quietness—in the midst of tumult.

Paul

You've rare ideas.

Princess

I wonder if you're not too prudent. I wonder if you want to go at all.

Paul

Why else should I have come?

Princess

You don't take me seriously. I wonder if you can find it in your conscience to work with me?

Paul

It isn't in my conscience I find it.

Princess

Never mind, I think I have you in my power.

Paul

You've got everyone in your power.

Princess

That extraordinary little sister of yours—surely you take her seriously?

Paul

I'm fond of her—if that's what you mean.

Princess

She's a prodigious person.

Paul

That she is—I don't see what interest you can have—

Princess

Interest in what?

Paul

In getting in so deep.

Princess (wryly)

Am I so deep?

Paul

Up to your pretty little neck. If I was your husband, I'd come and take you away.

Princess

You might find that difficult to do. Please, don't speak of my husband, you know nothing about him.

Paul

I know what Hyacinth has told me.

Princess

Oh, Hyacinth!

Paul

I don't have his manners.

Princess

I don't know that pretty manners are exactly what we're working for here. He's very foolish. He's deplorably conventional— Have you had a visit from Mr. Vetch?

Paul

The old gentleman who fiddles? No—he has never done me that honor.

Princess

You can thank me for that, I prevented him. He's in great

distress about Hyacinth—about the danger he's in. You know what I mean.

Paul

Yes, I know. Well?

Princess

He was going to you—to beg you to interfere— But, I prevented him.

Paul

That was considerate of you beyond everything.

Princess

It was not meant as consideration for you. It was a piece of calculation on my part. Do you know why I asked you to come and see me? Do you know why I went to see your sister? It was all part of a plan.

Paul

We thought it was all just ordinary upper class slumming.

Princess

Joke if you like. I wanted to save Hyacinth.

Paul

That's a fine idea.

Princess

I've no patience with his opinions. But, after all, it's not our friends' opinions that we love them for. I wanted you to help me get him out of his scrape.

Paul

His scrape isn't important.

Princess

They must be persuaded not to call him.

Paul

Persuade them, then, dear Madame.

Princess

How can I persuade them? I've no influence. Besides, my motives are suspect.

Paul

Shall I tell them he lacks the nerve?

Princess

He doesn't—he doesn't. Tell them he has changed his opinions.

Paul

That would be unwise. I don't wish to denounce him as a traitor.

Princess

Tell them it's simply my wish.

Paul

You're very fond of him. But, you ought to remember that, in the line you've chosen, our affections, our natural ties, our timidities, our shrinkings—all those things are as nothing. They must never weigh a feather beside our service.

Princess

Why don't you do his job for him?

Paul

Better to do my own.

Princess

And, what is that?

Paul

Don't know, I wait to be instructed.

Princess

Have you taken an oath too?

Paul

Ah, Madame, the oaths I take, I don't tell.

Princess

Can you see your comrade destroyed like that?

Paul

You had better leave my comrade to me.

Princess (with irritation)

Well then, shall we go?

Paul

If all this was only a pretext?

Princess (scornfully)

I believe you are afraid!

BLACKOUT

ACT V

Scene 12. The Same, a Few Days Later

The Princess is seated at her table, writing. Enter Hyacinth.

Hyacinth

I saw Lady Aurora leaving.

Princess

It's a pity that you didn't come a little sooner. You'd have assisted at a scene.

Hyacinth

At a scene?

Princess

She made a scene of tears. Perfectly well meant. She thinks I go too far.

Hyacinth

I imagine you tell her things you don't tell me.

Princess

Oh, you, my dear fellow.

Hyacinth

You've been going to some queer holes lately.

Princess

With your sentiments, you've no right to enquire.

Hyacinth

Don't you think so?

Princess

You mean your famous pledge to "act"? That will never come to anything.

Hyacinth

Why not, if you please?

Princess

It's too absurd, it's too vague. You won't have to do it.

Hyacinth (a little offended)

I think you mean I won't do it.

Princess (bluntly)

Well, then, you won't do it.

Hyacinth

You will—at the pace you're going.

Princess

What do you know about it? You're not worthy to know.

Hyacinth

You do go too far.

Princess

Of course, I do. How else does one know one's gone far enough? Lady Aurora's an angel, but she isn't the least in it, is she?

Hyacinth

Hardly.

Princess (troubled)

How can one go too far these days? That's the word of cowards.

Hyacinth

You think Lady Aurora's a coward?

Princess

Yes—in not having the courage of her opinions. The way the English can go half way to a thing, then stick in the middle!

Hyacinth

That's not your weakness, certainly! But the thing Lady Aurora's most afraid of is you!

Princess

There's one thing she's not afraid of. She'd marry your friend, Mr. Paul Muniment.

Hyacinth

Do you really think so?

Princess

She adores the ground he walks on.

Hyacinth

What would Belgrave Square and Inglefield say?

Princess

What they say already—that she's crazy. She'd do it in a minute. It would be fine to see it. It would be magnificent.

Hyacinth

She cannot marry him unless he asks her—she has not gone that far. And perhaps he won't.

Princess (wryly)

I don't think he will. Why haven't you been to see me lately?

Hyacinth

I knew you were deep in business.

Princess

And, you think it's all a mistake? Yes, I know that. If you were scared of me three or four months ago, I don't know what you'd think today. If you knew! I've risked everything.

Hyacinth

Fortunately, I don't know anything.

Princess

Why are you avoiding Paul and Rosy?

Hyacinth

It's no use keeping up pretenses. Our views are so different.

Princess

And, you are so grimly sincere! But, you could see Rosy—her views and yours coincide remarkably.

Hyacinth

I don't like Rosy.

Princess

Neither do I. Aren't you going to be in a fix when the hour strikes, and you're called upon to fulfill your vow?

Hyacinth

I'm in an awful fix. But, you just said it won't happen.

Princess

I pity you, my poor friend. I can imagine nothing more terrible than to find yourself face to face with your obligation—and the spirit that prompted you to undertake it dead within you.

Hyacinth

Terrible, indeed, Princess.

Princess

I pray to God it may never be your fate. You know, a short time ago, I had a visit from Mr. Vetch.

Hyacinth

It was kind of you to see him.

Princess

Any friend of yours— But he's delightful, I assure you. Do you know he came to me to beg me to snatch you away?

Hyacinth

From the danger that hangs over me?

Princess

He was most touching.

Hyacinth (affectionately)

He's a good old man.

Princess

He has a rather flattering belief in my personal effect on you.

Hyacinth

And he thought you'd try to get me to back out? He does you an injustice: you won't.

Princess

Because I know you won't be called.

Hyacinth

How do you know that?

Princess

Paul keeps me informed. We've information, my poor, dear boy. You're so much out of it, that if I told you, I fear you wouldn't understand.

Hyacinth

Yes, I'm out of it—but I still take as much of an interest in the real business as I ever did.

Princess

Dear, infatuated little aristocrat—was that ever very much?

Hyacinth

It was—and still is enough. I abide by the decision of others. I don't have to agree.

Princess

But you must. The old ferocious selfishness of the upper classes must come down. They won't leave gracefully, so they must be ushered out.

Hyacinth

I wish to God I could see it the way you see it.

Princess

What we're doing is at least worth trying. If those in power lack the will or the brains to think out a peaceful solution—on their heads be the blood!

Hyacinth

Princess, dearest Princess, if anything should happen to you!

Princess

To me! And pray, why not to me? What title have I to an exemption? Why am I so sacrosanct and so precious?

Hyacinth

Because there's no one in the world, and never has been anyone in the world, like you.

Princess

Oh, thank you!

BLACKOUT

ACT V

Scene 13. The Same, a Few Days Later

The Princess is in a negligee, smoking a cigarette. Paul, dressed only in pants and slippers, sits on the couch.

Paul

I've received a letter from your husband.

Princess

How in the world could he know your address?

Paul

Madame Grandoni, I think. He must have met her in Paris.

Princess

What an incorrigible cad.

Paul

I don't see that for writing to me. Would you like to see his letter?

Princess

Thank you, no. Nothing could induce me to touch anything he has touched.

Paul

You touch his money, my dear lady.

Princess

Because it makes him suffer.

Paul

I should think it would please him.

Princess

Why?

Paul

Because it shows you are dependent on him.

Princess

Not when he knows I don't use it for myself. He hates my politics almost as much as he hates me.

Paul

He doesn't hate you. His letter satisfies me of that.

Princess (facing him)

What are you leading up to? Are you suggesting I go back to my husband?

Paul

I don't know that I'd go so far as to advise it. But I believe you will before long.

Princess (really nettled)

And on what does that extraordinary prediction rest?

Paul

Because you'll soon have nothing to live on. He informs me that I need count on no more supplies from your hands.

Princess

He addresses you in very plain terms.

Paul

Yes.

Princess

And can you repeat such insults to me without the smallest apparent discomposure? You are indeed the most extraordinary man!

Paul

Why is it an insult? It's the simple truth—I take your money.

Princess

You take it for the cause—you don't take it for yourself.

Paul

Your husband isn't obliged to consider that.

Princess (bitingly)

I didn't know you were on his side!

Paul

You know whose side I'm on.

Princess

What does he know? What business has he to address you so?

Paul

Madame Grandoni has told him I have great influence with you.

Princess

She was welcome to tell him that!

Paul

He reasons that when I find you have nothing to give, I'll let you go.

Princess

Noting more to give. Does he think I count for nothing?

Paul

Apparently he thinks I don't count you much.

Princess (bitterly)

Well, I've always known you care more for my money than for me. But that's as it should be for a revolutionary. It makes no difference to me.

Paul (enjoying irritating her)

Then, by your own calculation, the Prince is right.

Princess

My dear sir, my interest in you never depended on your interest in me— So, he stops my allowance.

Paul

From the first of next month.

Princess

I'll fight him tooth and nail in court.

Paul

How? Your association with me and the Cause are not the sort of things that should come to light.

Princess

Why should it come to light? It's my money—separation money. What I do with it—

Paul

He can produce the fact that you had a little bookbinder living in your house.

Princess

What has that to do with it?

Paul

That would be for the court to appreciate. And, what about the fact that Madame Grandoni has withdrawn her protection?

Princess

Ah, but not for Hyacinth!

Paul

That's only a detail. In any case, I shouldn't in the least care to have you going to law.

Princess

Sometimes you seem afraid! That's terribly against your being a first rate man.

Paul

I haven't the smallest pretension of being a first rate man.

Princess

Oh, you're deep—and you're provoking!

Paul

Don't you remember how you accused me of being a coward and a traitor, of playing false, of wanting to back out?

Princess

Most distinctly! How can I help feeling that you've got incalculable ulterior motives and are consummately using me—consummately using us all?— Well, I don't care!

Paul

The best reason in the world for not going to law with your husband is this: When you haven't a penny left, you'll be obliged to go back and live with him.

Princess

How can that be? Haven't I my own property?

Paul

The Prince assures me that you've almost nothing left.

Princess

You've the most extraordinary tone. You seem to be saying that from the moment I have no more money to give you, I'm of no more value than the washed out tea leaves in that pot?

Paul

I've no intention of saying anything so offensive—but since you bring it up, perhaps it's as well I should let you know that I believe in giving your money or rather your husband's money to our business, you gave the most valuable thing you had to contribute.

Princess

This is the day of plain truths! You don't count my devotion or my intelligence—even rating my faculties modestly?

Paul

I count your intelligence but not your devotion. You are not trusted—well, where it makes the difference.

Princess

Not trusted! Why, I could be hanged tomorrow.

Paul

They may let you hang—without fully trusting you. You are likely to weary of us, and I think, you're weary even now.

Princess

Ah, you must be a first rate man—you're such a brute.

Paul

I didn't say you were weary of me. But you can never live poor. You don't begin to know the meaning of it.

Princess

Oh, no. I'm not tired of you! In a moment you'll make me cry with rage—and no man has done that for years. I was very poor when I was a girl.

Paul (unconvinced)

You'll go back to your husband.

Princess

I don't see why they trust you more than they do me?

Paul

I'm not sure they do. I've heard something this evening that suggests that.

Princess

And, may one know what it is?

Paul

A communication that should have been made through me was made through someone else.

Princess

A communication?

Paul

To Hyacinth.

Princess (uneasily)

To Hyacinth—?

Paul

He has his orders. But they didn't entrust it to me.

Princess

He was here this morning. Do you suppose he already had it?

Paul

Shinkel carried the order to him Sunday night.

Princess

But, he was here just now, and he told me nothing of it.

Paul

That was quite right of him.

Princess

What do they want him to do?

Paul

I think I'd better not tell you until it's over.

Princess

And when will it be over?

Paul

He has several days. He has considerable discretion as to seizing his chance. The thing's remarkably easy for him. I heard it all from Shinkel.

Princess

Shinkel trusts you, then?

Paul

Yes, but he won't trust you. Hyacinth has an invitation to a party at a country house. At a grand party, he'll fit right in—perfect gentleman.

Princess (tartly)

He'll like that.

Paul

If he doesn't like it, he needn't do it.

Princess

And the target?

Paul

A certain royal personage. Do you want to warn him?

Princess

By no means. But I prefer to do the business myself.

Paul

To fall by your beautiful hand would be too good for him.

Princess

However if he fails, it will be useful, valuable?

Paul

It's worth trying, even if it fails. He's a very bad institution, although as a private person, quite blameless.

Princess

And, you don't mean to go near Hyacinth?

Paul

I mean to leave him free.

(Pause.)

Princess

Paul Muniment, you are a truly first rate man! Why have you told me this?

Paul

So that you can't throw it up to me later that I didn't.

Princess

What will Hyacinth do?

Paul

I don't know. He'll either kill himself if he can't go through with it—or he'll kill The Grand Duke.

Princess

God! I must talk to him.

Paul

No. If Hyacinth fails or funks it, then it's your chance. There's a second party.

Princess

God—poor Hyacinth. What will he do? What will he do? Oh, it's my fault. It's through me that he's changed his ideas.

Paul

But, not because of you, really. You've always stood for the Cause.

Princess

Yes, but I showed him the other side—

Paul

That cannot be helped.

Princess

I wish I hadn't said some of the things I said to him this morning. I told him I didn't think he'd do it. He was talking to me, trying to tell me without actually telling me. It was his swan song. I should have known, but I was caught up in my own egotism, I was so smug.

Paul

There's nothing to do but wait and see.

Princess

He's only a child. A poor deluded child.

Paul

If he weren't a man, he'd have run away. He won't run. He'll either do it, or he'll destroy himself.

Princess

I don't think he can do it. I don't believe he can do it. (bursting into tears)

Paul (after a moment)

I don't mean to aggravate you, but you will go back to your husband.

(The Princess shakes her head at Paul, they stare at each other as the Curtain falls.)

CURTAIN

ABOUT THE AUTHOR

Frank J. Morlock has written and translated many plays since retiring from the legal profession in 1992. His translations have also appeared on Project Gutenberg, the Alexandre Dumas Père web page, Literature in the Age of Napoléon, Infinite Artistries.com, and Munsey's (formerly Blackmask). In 2006 he received an award from the North American Jules Verne Society for his translations of Verne's plays. He lives and works in México.

www.ingramcontent.com/pod-product-compliance
Lightning Source LLC
LaVergne TN
LVHW041616070426
835507LV00008B/283